With an Introduction by Robert Hass

Ten Thousand
lives

Ko Un

Translated by Brother Anthony of Taizé,
Young-moo Kim, and Gary Gach

GREEN INTEGER
KØBENHAVN & LOS ANGELES
2005

GREEN INTEGER BOOKS
Edited by Per Bregne
København / Los Angeles

Distributed in the United States by Consortium Book
Sales and Distribution, 1045 Westgate Drive, Suite 90
Saint Paul, Minnesota 55114-1065
Distributed in England and Europe by
Turnaround Publisher Services
Unit 3, Olympia Trading Estate
Coburg Road, Wood Green, London N22 6TZ
44 (0)20 88293009

First published by Green Integer 2005
Originally published in Korea as *Maninbo*, Volumes 1-3 (1986),
Volumes 4-7 (1988), Volumes 8-9 (1989), Volume 10 (1996)
Copyright ©1986, 1988, 1989, 1996 by Ko Un
Published by agreement with Ko Un
Introduction copyright ©2005 by Robert Hass
English language translation copyright ©2005 by Brother Anthony of Taizé,
Young-moo Kim, and Gary Gach
Back cover copy ©2005 by Green Integer
All rights reserved

The translators would like the thank the editors of the following journals and books
in which some of these poems first appeared: *Americas Review, The Heart as Origami*
(Rising Fire Press), *Korean Culture, The London Magazine, Manoa, New American
Writing, The Sound of My Waves* (Cornell-DapGae), and *The Stony Thursday Book.* Thanks
also to Neela Banerjee whose interview with the poet in winter 2001 furnished valuable
reference material. The translators gratefully acknowledge the support received from the
Korean Culture and Arts Foundation. The publication of this book was supported by a gen-
erous grant from the Korea Literature Translation Institute, Seoul, Korea.

Design: Per Bregne
Typography: Kim Silva
Cover photograph: Ko Un

LIBRARY OF CONGRESS CATALOGING IN PUBLICATION DATA
Ko Un [1933]
Ten Thousand Lives
ISBN: 1-933382-06-6
p. cm – Green Integer 123
I. Title II. Series III. Translators
Green Integer books are published for Douglas Messerli

Contents

On Ko Un and *Maninbo*

I first became aware of Ko Un in 1986, when I was in Seoul, Korea for a conference of PEN, the international literary organization. Writers from all over the world had gathered to discuss issues of censorship and freedom of speech. One night I was taken to a local university campus, where there was an evening of poetry and music. These were the last years of the succession of military dictatorships which had ruled the Republic of Korea since the end of the Korean War. The reading was sponsored by a student democracy movement which also supported the re-unification of Korea, though it was a crime in those years to mention the possibility in public. That night the air was charged with the energy that precedes a political breakthrough: it felt more like a political rally than a poetry reading. As the students sang and read their poems, my attention was drawn to a wiry, vigorous man on the back of the stage, gray-haired, barefoot, dressed like a peasant farmer, who was pounding a traditional Korean drum. There was something enormously graceful and droll in his movements, and my eyes kept drifting back to him. He seemed to be having a wonderful time. Finally I turned to my guide, a Korean novelist. "Who is that guy whacking the drum?" "That," he said, "is the best poet in the Korean language." My first sighting of Ko Un.

The first volume of *Maninbo,* or *Ten Thousand Lives,* must have just been published that spring. The story of its genesis has the quality of legend. Ko Un was born in 1933 and attended school under a Japanese colonial administration that outlawed the teaching of the Korean language in Korean schools. He studied Chinese classics at a village school, and learned to read and write Korean surreptitiously from a neighbor's servant. He escaped combat in the Korean War because he was so thin the army would not draft him, but the good luck of his early malnourishment did not save him from witnessing its extraordinary violence. One of his jobs at the end of the war was transporting corpses to their burial places, after which he had a portside job with the U.S. Army keeping track of the unloaded munitions that were doing the killing. At nineteen he entered a Son (Zen) Buddhist monastery and threw himself into the rigors of Son training. He published his first book of poems in 1960. In 1963 he wrote an essay disavowing monastic life and denouncing its laxness and corruption. He lived in Seoul for a while, taught school on a remote island where he established a public high school, and by his own account was as drunk as possible as much as possible. He also read existentialist philosophy, and tormented himself with the nothingness of existence while he wrote essays and poems that expressed his restlessness and torment.

Sometime in the early 1970's something in him changed and he became, within a few years, one of the leading figures in the resistance movement against the Republic's military dictatorships. He was imprisoned four times, tortured, as a result of which he lost the hearing on one ear, and during his third imprisonment in 1980, when he had been sentenced to 20 years in prison, while in solitary confinement in a cell so pitch dark he could not see the glint of the coffee can that served as a latrine, he began to make a mental inventory of the faces of everyone he had ever known and conceived a long poem, or series of poems, that would begin in his childhood village and expand to include everyone he had ever met, including figures vivid to him from history and literature. The project, still ongoing, has reached twenty volumes and this book is the first full sampling of it to appear in English translation.

Ko Un was released from prison on the occasion of a general pardon in 1982. In 1983 he was married, for the first time, at the age of 50, to Lee Sangwha, a professor of English literature. They settled in the country two hours outside of Seoul and they had a daughter in 1985. Ko Un, always prolific, set to work on the *Maninbo*. He also produced *Paektu Mountain*, a narrative poem in seven volumes on the Korean independence movement against Japanese rule, a best-selling novel *The Garland Sutra* in 1991, and several books of small, aphoristic Son poems, which return his poetry to its youthful roots in Buddhist practice. In the midst of this immense productivity he had plunged into the movement for the reunification of the Korean peninsula, becoming Chairman of the Association of Korean Artists from 1989-1990 and President of the Association of Writers for National Literature from 1992 to 1994. In 1989, as a symbolic act, he attempted to visit North Korea without government permission and was jailed a final time for two months. In his introduction to the translation of Ko Un's Buddhist poems, Allen Ginsberg describes him as "a jailbird," a title he has earned, and also as "a demon-driven Bodhisattva of Korean poetry, exuberant, demotic, abundant, obsessed with poetic creation."

There was not much of Ko Un to be read in English in 1986, or of any other contemporary Korean poet. The one easily available volume, *The Silence of Love: Twentieth Century Korean Poetry*, though it included several very interesting contemporary poets, did not include him. It was published in 1980 when he was in jail. Since that time two volumes of his work have appeared: *The Sound of My Waves: Selected Poems of Ko Un*, translated by Brother Anthony of Taizé and Young-moo Kim and published in the Cornell East Asia Series in 1996, and *Beyond Self: 108 Korean Zen Poems*, also translated by Brother Anthony and Prof. Kim, and published by Parallax Press in 1997.

Reading him and thinking about Korean poetry, I realized that even though the lives and fates of the American and Korean peoples have been intertwined for the last half century, American readers knew almost nothing about Korean culture and still less about Korean poetry. The one study of classical Korean poetry in English, *The Bamboo Grove: An Introduction to Sijo,* published in 1971 by Richard Rutt, an Anglican bishop living in Korea, provides a way in. *Sijo* is the classical Korean song form; it consists of three fourteen syllable lines—long lines, that tended to break in half, so that the translations seem to turn naturally enough into five- and six-line poems in English. Here is a poem from the sixteenth century that has some of the qualities of Chinese Buddhist work. It comes from a group of poems called *The Nine Songs of Ko San:*

Where shall we find the ninth song?
Winter has come to Munsan;
The fantastic rocks are buried under snow.
Nobody comes here for pleasure now.
They think there is nothing to see.

And this poem from the eighteenth century has one of Ko Un's themes and something of his colloquial pungency:

A boy comes by my window
  shouting that it's New Year's.
I open the eastern lattice—
  the usual sun has risen again
See here, boy! It's the same old sun.
  Come tell me when a new one dawns!

Let me juxtapose this to a passage from the preface Ko Un wrote in 1993 to the volume which appeared in English under the title *Beyond Self: 108 Korean Zen Poems:*

The whole world renewed! I want to offer water to all who thirst for a new world. I want to light a fire so they can warm themselves on a cold evening. I long to give them bars of iron to hold on to, to prevent them from being swept away by raging storms. But people made of mud cannot cross streams, people made of wood cannot go near a fire. And people made of iron will rust away in less than a century.

Here stand a good-for-nothing who let himself get soaked until the mud dissolved, set fire to himself so the wood disappeared, and whose iron finally rusted away in the wind and the rain. Go now. The new world is found wherever new life comes to birth.

The hopefulness in this, and the bardic sense of responsibility, and the irony and the absence of irony seem to belong to a particular kind of historical moment. They put me in mind, because of my long experience of translating Polish poetry, of something Czeslaw Milosz said: "Woe to the poet born to an interesting piece of geography in a violent time."

The parallels between the geographic and cultural situations of Poland and Korea are very striking. Given their long histories as the playgrounds of imperial powers and the kind of suffering that has come from it and the impact it's had on poetry, I don't think it's an accident that important work in poetry in this last half century has come from Poland and Korea. Such suffering is not a fate anyone wishes on anyone else and it doesn't mean that every time there is a catastrophe, poetry rises to the occasion. But in the case of Korea, it seems to have done so in interesting ways. The reason is not, I think, because it is dramatic to live inside violence or terrible injustice, but because it is numbing and that numbing incites a spirit of resistance. Not only were limitations placed on the Korean literary tradition by the immense human suffering of the war years, there was also an active pressure by the Japanese colonizers between 1910 and 1945 to eradicate Korean culture.

Milosz has said that the difficulty with writing in Polish was that, for historical reasons, the blossom of every tree in a Polish poem was a Polish blossom. My sense is that something quite similar happened to Korean poetry. Because the Japanese spent almost fifty years trying to extinguish Korean culture, the pressure to preserve a national tradition must have been enormous—and, in some ways, deeply conservative. On the other hand, Korean poetry had opened itself to the influence of the West, particularly to French poetry, just as Japanese poetry had, and a sort of symbolist lyric entered Korean literature. And the mix of a modernizing idiom with colonialism must have been complicated for poets to negotiate. My impression is that the best early twentieth century Korean poets tried to solve the problem by fusing the symbolist lyric formally with the folk tradition. But that lyric itself was transformed by the historical situation, so that a certain delicacy and intense melancholy in the late nineteenth century French poems, which was not particularly political in French, was quite political in Korean.

The vagueness of French symbolist poetry, its desire to detach word from thing, to give the mind a little room to float and make up new values, was in only that broad sense political in French poetry. In Korean, however, especially in early modern Korean poetry, suggestiveness became a kind of code which could both acknowledge and subvert a severe censorship. This was apparently intensified by the use of rhythms that echoed a folk tradition, so there was a struggle inside poetry between the old and the new, in a situation which might have caused any writer to feel ambivalent about both. In such a literary moment, somebody has to be the dog that bites through the leash; somebody has to be the one who says what has to be said. If those who do it are also artists of enduring power, they will find ways of refocusing the lens of a tradition. Reading Korean poetry in translation, reading through the evolution of Ko Un from the early poems to the *Mainibo*, it struck me that this is what must have happened in his case.

It is also very striking to see the kind of tuning fork he has been, reinventing himself in every decade through the turns in Korea's postwar political and social history. In his early work, it's my impression that he was writing in some version of the received tradition of Korean nature lyric with symbolist overtones, touched by the Korean folk tradition, touched by Son Buddhism, which, compared to the sense of refinement in Zen Buddhist poetry, seems earthy and intellectually tough. In the period from 1962 to 1973, less well documented in the existing translations, after he left his life as a monk, the poetry seems to change. The vision of this work is dark, but the poems themselves have a sense of naturalness and spontaneity, even a cultivated raggedness, not unlike American experimental poetry of the same period. Between 1973 and his imprisonment in 1980 was a period of intense political involvement. It can be a disaster artistically for a poet to write an explicitly engaged political poetry, however morally admirable the impulse is, and the wariness of poets is well-founded.

Ko Un, like Whitman or Neruda, seems to have had no aesthetic difficulties with the idea of giving himself and the trajectory of his art to a national project. The project had several elements. One was resistance to censorship. A deeper one was resistance to the series of military dictatorships underwritten by the United States. And the third was an intense longing—necessarily metaphorical in the culture of the Republic—for the final healing of the wounds of colonialism and war that would come from the reunification of his country. The poet who had thrown himself into this project was the one I'd seen that night pounding the drum on the stage at the University. *Mainibo* seems to have been his way of turning the quarrel inside the Korean literary tradition into poetry. A Korean critic, Choi Won-shik, described it this way: "The unique space where anti-traditional modernism and anti-western traditionalism meet is where the poetry of Ko Un originates."

Here's a poem from Ko Un's first book, published in 1960. It's called "Sleep":

No matter how deeply I sleep
The moonlit night
Remains as bright as ever.

If I wake with a start
Turn
And nestle down again

Once my eyes have closed
The moonlight trapped inside them
Becomes part of me.

But are the clouds washed pure?
Pure enough for the moon
As it drops behind the western hills?

Now my sleep is a shadow of sleep,
A shadow cast on a moonlit night.

(tr. Brother Anthony of Taizé and Young-moo Kim)

This is an inward poem, quietly beautiful. As English readers, we're deprived of any sense of what its verbal and stylistics resonances are in Korean. It sounds like mid-century American free verse, put to the use of plainness or clarity. The sensation of the sleeper, having opened his eyes and closed them with a feeling that he was still holding the moonlight, is exquisite. The turn in the poem—the shadow cast by the hunger for an entire purity—seems Rilkean. It is beautiful and one recognizes beauty.

Here is a poem from 1974 called "Destruction of Life":

Cut off parents, cut off children!
This and that and this not that
And anything else as well
Cut off and dispatch by the sharp blade of night.
Every morning heaven and earth
Are piled with dead things.
Our job is to bury them all day long.

(tr. Brother Anthony of Taizé and Young-moo Kim)

This has, to my ear, the toughmindedness of Korean Buddhism and the kind of raggedness and anger I associate with American poetry in the 1950's and 60's, the young Allen Ginsberg or Leroi Jones. I've read that Korean poetry is not so aesthetically minded as Japanese poetry partly because it stayed closer to oral traditions rather than traditions of learning, which may be what gives this poem its quality. It's more demotic than "Sleep," more spontaneous and tougher, less satisfied to rest in beauty.

Maninbo seems to flow from a fusion of these traditions. For anyone who has spent even a little time in Korea, the world that springs to life in these poems is instantly recognizable, and for anyone who has tried to imagine the war years and the desperate poverty that came after, these poems will seem to attend to a whole people's experience and to speak from it. Not surprisingly, hunger is at the center of the early volumes. Their point of view is the point of view of the village, their way of speaking about the shapes of lives the stuff of village gossip. They are even, at moments, the street seen with a child's eyes so that characters come on stage bearing a ten year old's sense of a neighborhod's Homeric epithets: the boy with two cowlicks, the fat, mean lady in the corner house. The poems have that intimacy. Most of them are as lean as the village dogs they describe; in hard times people's characters seem to stand out like their bones and the stories in the poems have therefore a bony and synoptic clarity. Terrifying legends of cannibalism are one moral pole of this world and a sweet and clearminded kindness is another. The stories are as pungent as kimchee and one of the things that gives them their poignancy is the wide net they cast. We are always aware that their social world is defined by an individual's effort to recall every life that has touched his, to make a map of the world that way. It's what makes an early poem in the sequence, "The Women from Sŏnjei-ri" so affecting. Here's the beginning of it:

In darkest night, near midnight, the dogs
in the middle of Saet'ŏ begin their raucous barking.
One dog barks, so the next one barks
until the dogs at Kalmoe across the fields
follow suit and start barking as well.
Between the barking of the dogs,
scraps of voices echo: *eh ah oh*…
Not unlike the sound the night's wild geese
Let fall upon the bitter cold ground
as they fly over, high above,
not unlike that splendid sound
echoing back and forth.
It's the women from Sŏnjei-ri on their way home
from the old-style market over at Kunsan
where they'd gone with garlic bulbs by the hundreds

in baskets on their heads,
there being a lack of *kimchi* cabbages
from the bean fields.
Now they're on their way home,
after getting rid of what couldn't be sold
at the clearing auction at closing time—
several miles gone,
several miles left to go in deepest night!

It's hard to think of analogues for this work. The sensibility, alert, instinctively democratic, comic, unsentimental, is a little like William Carlos Williams; the project is a little like Edgar Lee Masters' *Spoon River Anthology* or the more political and encyclopedic ambitions of Charles Reznikoff's *Testimony*. The point of view and the overheard quality remind me of the Norwegian poet Paal-Helge Haugen's *Stone Fences,* a delicious book that calls up the whole social world of the Cold War and the 1950's from the point of view of a child in a farming village. For the dark places the poems are willing to go, they can seem in individual poems a little like the narratives of Robert Frost, but neither Masters's work nor Frost's has Ko Un's combination of pungent village gossip and epic reach. Even with this generous selection of poems, we do not have the whole shape of the work in hand, and perhaps it is enough to notice the fertility of Ko Un's poetic resources. One would think that the poems would begin to seem formulaic, that the ways of calling up a life would begin to be repetitive, and they never are. In that way it is a book of wonders in its mix of the lives of ordinary people, people from stories and legends, and historical figures. They all take their place inside this extraordinarily rich reach of a single consciousness.

Ko Un is a remarkable poet and one of the heroes of human freedom in this half-century. One hesitates to say this in an introduction to his poems, because American readers have often been drawn to poetry in translation because of the dramatic political circumstances that produced it rather than by the qualities of the work iself. But no one who begins to read this book will doubt that what matters here is the work itself. *Maninbo* is one of the most extraordinary projects in contemporary literature and it is a very good thing to have these poems in English. For that we owe gratitude to Brother Anthony of Taizé and Young-moo Kim for their now more than a decade's devotion to getting this work into English, and to Gary Gach who, after Mr. Kim's death, joined Brother Anthony to give these poems their freshness and naturalness in English.

— ROBERT HASS

The Background People:
A Translators' Preface

When Ko Un draws the Chinese word for person (*ren*), he observes how it leans slightly. Thus he notes human relationship is interdependent. We all live in relationship between people. From the time we're born, we meet so many people. It's his obligation as poet to mark each encounter. Indeed, even a passing stranger is cause for celebration.

How Ko Un came to commemorate so many stories in such an amazing project of cultural memory is bound up with his own story, which Robert Hass relates so well herein. He was born in 1933 in a small rural village on the outskirts of the port town of Kunsan, in Korea's North Cholla Province. He grew up in a Korea that had been annexed by Japan in 1910, where all education and official business were conducted entirely in Japanese, and from which any mention of Korea's distinct history had been banished. Liberation from Japanese colonization came with the end of the Second World War in 1945, but the country was in a state of dire poverty and soon fell prey to fierce power struggles that quickly became part of the much wider Cold War. In June 1950, the army of Communist North Korea invaded the South, which had declared itself a republic in 1948, launching the Korean War, which as of this writing has never officially ended.

Ko Un became a Buddhist monk in 1952, following military conscription, where he'd experienced the horrors of war. He published his first poems in 1958, to considerable recognition, while still a monk. He became himself a master and attained high rank in the monastic order, yet disrobed in 1962, returning to secular life.

During the 1970s, he became a leading spokesman in the struggle for freedom and democracy, for which the military regime often arrested and imprisoned him. In May 1980, in the run up to the coup d'état led by Chun Doo-Hwan, he was arrested along with hundreds of other dissidents. Thrown into military prisons, they were tried in arbitrary court martials. Ko Un was sentenced to 20 years imprisonment for rebellion.

He describes the prison in which they were kept as a labyrinth of tiny, windowless cells lit only by one small electric bulb. Completely isolated from the world and, most of the time, from one another, they had no way of knowing if they would ever come out alive or be summarily executed and disappear without trace. In that dark prison, in such a dark time, Ko Un's Buddhist training helped sustain him. And he reflected deeply on the significance of his vocation as poet, its connection with Korean history. In so doing, he felt a deep connection between his own sufferings and those of the many Koreans he'd encountered in his life, either directly or in the pages of books. He felt called to promise them that, if ever he came out alive, he would set about writing a poetic record of the life of every person he'd ever known or known of. He found he could let events take their course; even if he was destined to die, the very fact of having made this vow was enough.

He and the others arrested with him were released in 1982, as soon as the dictatorial regime of the former general Chun Doo-hwan felt confident of their control over the country. However, Ko Un couldn't immediately begin to fulfill his promise, for in the following months came his marriage and the move away from Seoul to a house in a quiet rural setting in Ansong, almost two hours' bus ride to the south. It was late in 1986 that the first volume of *Maninbo* was published; further volumes have followed over the years. Volume 20 was published in 2004, and he plans for another five volumes before bringing the project to a close. It might be noted that *Maninbo* is but part of possibly the most prolific output of any contemporary Korean author. Current estimates peg his complete works as comprising close to 150 books thus far.

The title *Maninbo* means, literally "family records of ten thousand lives." He's hoped that, in Korean at least, it might, in part, evoke the idea of "the background people," as he once put it. Another reading of *Maninbo* could be "all the people." And thus an alternate view of history takes shape, by its bootstraps, as it were.

The early entries are mainly dedicated to people he knew in his childhood, his relatives, simple village families, his teachers. More recently, he's begun to depict the dissidents with whom whom he was so active under the military dictatorships.

Our selection contains some of the finest poems

from the first ten volumes. They were chosen by Young-moo Kim, and it is a source of great regret that his premature death in 2001 prevented him writing a critical commentary for this volume. We dedicate this edition to the memory of our dear colleague.

The Translators

Brother Anthony of Taizé is a professor in the English Department at Sogang University, Seoul, where he has been teaching Medieval and Renaissance English literature and culture since the 1980s. He is also a renowned translator of modern Korean literature. Born in England, he is now a Korean national with the name An Sonjae.

Homepage: http://www.sogang.ac.kr/~anthony

The late Young-moo Kim, (1944-2001) was a Professor of English Literature at Seoul National University, and was well known in Korea as a literary critic and poet. He published three volumes of his own poetry. With Brother Anthony, he's translated and published poems by Ch'on Sang-pyong, Kim Kwang-kyu, So Chong-ju, Kim Su-young, Lee Si-young and Shin Kyong-nim, as well as Ko Un.

Gary Gach is the author of six books, He's also editor of *What Book!? : Buddha Poems from Beat to Hiphop* (American Book Award, 1999), which includes three poems by Ko Un, his first encounter with this force of nature. Homepage: http://word.to

Volume I (1986)

Grandfather

Even when he's drunk himself into a stupor,
there are two things he skillfully keeps from slipping —
the tongue in his mouth
and the long pipe sticking out of the collar of his jacket.
If he collapses and passes out on a rice-field bank
because of the great power of a gallon of *makkŏlli*,
his three sons come running, as good sons should,
and home he comes, borne on their shoulders.
Once back home, he demands another drink, smashes
    the fence down,
shouts out to the neighborhood, everywhere
    and nowhere,
as far as the red-clay fields of the next village
struck by lightning not so long ago,
then falls asleep, screaming, "Bitch bitch! Bitch!"
Once he comes round, he's fresh water's blood-brother.
There he is, standing with folded arms, the butt
    of scolding
under the rainwater falling from the eaves, Ko Han-gil.

Perhaps gaining enlightenment thereby?
"Kid, remember, Japan is not our country.
Back in the old days, Admiral Yi Sun-shin gave the
    Japs hell.
So don't lose heart."
If his family was dizzy with hunger after missing
    several meals,
he'd kindle a fire in the kitchen so that the
    chimney smoked.
Deceiving anybody watching into thinking he was at least
    boiling gruel,
he'd boil plain water, burning fresh pine branches
that made smoke thick enough to choke on.

If an enemy of three years' standing offered him a drink,
    no problem —
wine was all his heaven and his fields.
He'd gaze out at the flourishing fields in the summer heat,
the rice paddies that all belonging to others,
    as the last
will-o'the-wisps of the year were rising.

While he was in the world he had a name, but when he
    passed away
there was no stone to inscribe his name on.
At memorial rites, they just write "A Student of Life" on
    the soul tablet.
Because he'd learned so much.
He'd learned so much.

Sam-man's Grandmother

Stories from days of old, long long ago,
the stories I heard while early mosquitoes bit my
    infant skin
in summer, as the crape-myrtle trees at Chungttŭm
blossomed in thick clusters of pink flowers…

"Long long ago an elderly bachelor and his old
    widowed mother
lived together in a village…"

Maybe Ch'olchong was king, or Kochong, no matter,
every tale was a tale beginning long long ago…
One day when snow was swirling down,
one endless day,
though the stove had gone out and the room was icy,
Sam-man's old grandmother with her broad pock-
    marked face
told a tale of an elderly bachelor of long long ago,
joining to it this time a tale of a spool of silk…

Long long ago a boy was living in a village.

His sister was carried off by brigands but
in that emergency she unrolled behind her a spool of
     silk so
he set out after her, following the thread over hills
     and streams
until it dropped ten fathoms into a well.
Descending to the bottom of that well he found a door
     in the rock
and *ah*, there lay another world.
While it was midwinter in our world, peach trees
     there were in flower.
He found his sister. She was due to become the bride
of the bandit leader the following day
in a wedding hall hung with red and blue lanterns.
"For goodness sakes! Let's go home, quick!"
He carried her home on his back over hills and streams.
She became the bride of a bachelor in the next village,
he married a moon-faced maid from the next village.
They ate well, lived well, survived to a ripe old age
of one hundred and eighty-five. So the story went.
She was such a great storyteller, she would bewitch
     our eyes.
We kids used to glimpse the whole wide world in her
     blackberry-black eyes.

When she died, it seemed she was eager to go on
    telling tales,
because she died with her mouth wide open
and no matter how hard they tried to close it, it kept
    falling open again.

The Peddler of Bamboo Crates*

A peddler used to visit farmhand Tae-gil's room.
On his back, he'd transport bamboo crates and baskets
   from the south
to the northernmost point on the Yalu River,
to the easternmost parts of the country,
to places where it gets so cold you freeze walking,
freeze, walking, then when spring comes your feet fall off.
That peddler roamed all over the land. In the end,
he lost all his money peddling bamboo baskets and crates.
Seeing him reduced to abject poverty,
Tae-gil readily gave him a year of his own wages as a loan.
"Come back and repay it this time next year."
The peddler set out, filled with delight.
One year passed, a second, with never a whisper of news.
"You see!? You see?!" —
everyone declared he'd let himself be robbed
but Tae-gil never turned so much as a hair,
just went on twisting cords of straw coiling higher
   and higher.

---

* Titles followed by an asterisk have notes attached (pages 350-364).

Then, years later, early one winter,
that peddler he'd loaned the money to showed up,
bringing with him a bottle of liquor and ten dried skate.
He produced the sum he owed from three years before,
    and more,
explaining how he'd travelled and travelled and only now
    got back,
and he was sorry.
Tae-gil replied: "You must have had a hard time."
"I'll drink to that."
"Now you're talking."

Delighted, Pok-gil the peddler downed one, hoped
    for another.
"Yes indeed, indeed, quite right!"

Sa-haeng

On a bank by the stream at Mijei
a solitary fisherman,
long-legged Sa-haeng,
was reeling in his line.
Sa-haeng's son Ch'il-song came running along the
  other bank.
"Dad, Dad! Ma's dead. She died and won't shut her eyes!"
He was too far away, his shouts were wasted.

Cold waves lap between the two, forever parted.

Our Great-Aunt at Taegi*

Whenever she arrives after making the five-mile journey
along the meadow paths from Taegi village,
our great-aunt takes up all the room.
The day grandmother died, she'd no sooner arrived
than she began to howl, rocking her great body from side
   to side.
She beat on the ground, she beat her thighs, and
   she howled:
"What on earth is this? What's happened to you?
Why, I met you at Hoihyŏn Market
and we ate thin noodles that had soaked in the broth
until they were swollen thick.
Another time we bought soup and rice,
with a measure of *makkŏlli* — it seems like only yesterday.
How fast those five or six years have passed.
Back last autumn
you were saying: In a few more months
this wretched sickness will be over
and I'll go flying about all over the place.
Now where have you gone flying away to? *Aigu*, sister,
   aigu, sister.

If you leave us, when will you ever return?
Life here is good, even if sometimes you find
  yourself stuck
in cowshit or dogshit,
but now you've gone to the world beyond
and in that great world beyond
where will you live, who will look after you?
Aigu," she shouted, "*aigu, aigu!*"
She went on and on lamenting, then wiped her running
  nose and
happening to glance behind, saw our second
  cousin's wife,
who'd come over from her new home in Songmal village.
Her laments were suddenly a thing of the past.
"*Aigu*, the bride from Songmal!
You look so well! What a beaming face!
How're the kids getting on?
I hear you've bought one more rice-field patch?
Good fortune came back after you dug your new well!"
What we call sorrow is not the least bit sad, really.
It's like a stream hidden in a valley, gone like the tune of
  a song
once you're over the crest of the next hill.

When a woman like her enters a house of mourning,
the wine and food in the offerings find their
    proper flavor,
don't they?

The Inn at the Road Junction*

Needless to say, there's an inn
at the junction where the road forks for Okjŏngkol
    and Chigok-ri,
at the point where
the road for Chaetjŏngji reluctantly turns off,
an inn where just a few gourd flowers bloom.
It's so spotlessly clean
you could easily use the bar as an altar for
    ancestor offerings.
A fly has not a second to settle anywhere.
Ok-son's the hostess,
slight of build, still young to look at, though nearly fifty.
When she serves a bowl of *makkŏlli*,
there's always a portion of ageing *kimch'i* to help it down.
For a few weeks in summer she serves garlic shoots
soaked in red-pepper paste.
She wipes and wipes the bar,
as if disaster might strike if her hands were idle.
If you overdo things, they say,
it drives good luck away.
She pays no heed to any such ideas,

merely says: "A lot of people frequent this place,
it would never do for it to be dirty."
That's the kind of inn it is,
good luck may go or stay as it likes.
From time to time, as the sun is about to set,
if there aren't many customers
she comes out to the junction
and gazes at a lonely tomb across from the inn:
"Ah, man from Little Village,
I'd do better to die soon myself."
She lingers a moment, then goes back to serving drinks.
On days when the smell of the water hangs especially heavy
along the river bank at Mijei,
she talks to the tomb for a while
as one more day grows dark.

Father

No matter how weary he was, plodding down roads,
across the river, all over Naep'o,
from Taech'ŏn market to Yesan market to Sŏsan market,
Father was a dreamer through and through.
When it rained,
he would hold out both hands to the rain
and exclaim in delight: "*Aigu, aigu!* How good to
    see you!"

Tears of Blood*

"My youngest son…if you want to be remembered by posterity,
you must serve your country."

Those words are spoken by Old Man Ch'oi
in the early modern novel *Tears of Blood*.
Yet its author, Lee In-jik, went to Japan on a scholarship,
learned Japanese, then served as an interpreter for the
    Japanese Army
during the Russo-Japanese War.
Later, he was a newspaper's editor-in-chief, then
    its chairman,
before becoming secretary and interpreter to
    Lee Wan-yong.
As such, he was the man who sold our nation
with its twenty million people
to the Japanese
for a mere thirty million *won*.
Lee Wan-yong's rival, Song Pyŏng-jun, had said
    the Japanese
should pay at least one hundred million,
but eager to gain credit for the annexation
he offered a closing bargain,
slashing the hundred million to a mere thirty.

In later years, Lee In-jik failed to get a single decoration.
He wrote occasional columns for the *Maeil Sinbo* paper,
then died, leaving *Tears of Blood* behind him.
He was cremated Japanese-style at Aogae Crematorium.
The four hundred and fifty *won* the Japanese authorities
paid to cover his funeral expenses were his sole reward
for having administered the annexation.
He was the main pioneer of the modern Korean novel.
After him tower the figures of Ch'oi Nam-sŏn and
    Lee Kwang-su.
Ah, scribblers of Korea, down on your knees in awe.

The Wife from Kwi Island

When I was four I followed my youngest uncle
five miles across fields reclaimed from the sea,
on and on until my little legs were buckling
by the time we reached the sea that went soaring up to
   the sky.
We waited until a muddy path lay uncovered at low tide
and there crossed over to Kwi Island,
where we met the boatman's wife,
his marvelous wife.
'Why, if he'd only lived, my kid would have been your age.
Take some of this with you, taste this, eat this.'
Her large greenish lips kept chattering
as she deftly hooked up a large skate.
That wife was no mere human, she was the very heart of
   the sea.
Later I climbed to the top of Halmi Hill and stared
for I don't know how long out toward the sea and the
   island wife.
And as I gazed my feet ached.

Aunt

That aunt of ours who married the man at Sŏrae Ferry
Aunt Ye-bok
her laugh
a laugh like cold bean-sprout soup
Aunt Ye-bok
that cold aunt who had wept her fill.

Do-sŏn the Snake-Catcher

Do-sŏn from Pangjuk hamlet, used to catch a snake,
skin it then and there, sprinkle it with salt,
and gobble it up merrily.
We found him creepy and ran away from him.
Wherever Do-sŏn the snake-catcher went,
vipers, yellow serpents, every kind of snake froze, helpless
at the sight of him, and let themselves be caught.
They were already caught before Do-sŏn impaled them
on his snake-catcher's stick with an awl fixed to its tip.
We used to run away, fearing to meet him in our dreams.
Yet he had a heart like an angel's.
If there was a death in a house he would do all
    the hard work,
wail and lament, of course, then lament again at
    the offerings
three days after the funeral.
He might be a snake-catcher, his heart was
    really sensitive…

Azaleas

Halmi Hill used to be ablaze with azaleas
until I was four years old.
After that, for several years running
we were reduced to grubbing out the azalea roots
and burning them to heat the rooms in winter.
Those were hard times.
There were no azaleas left to blossom when spring came.
If people were poor, it was only right
that Halmi Hill behind the village should also be poor.
Still, a few azalea roots survived
and soon they at least were blooming again.
Yang-gum, a girl from our village, climbed up to see
    those azaleas,
wearing a long red ribbon,
piled stones around them and built a fence,
forgot home and tasks for a while, just sat there.
"Gosh! What am I doing, still here? Gracious,
    goodness gracious!"

Kojumong: The Founder of Koguryŏ *

"Go.
Go and found your kingdom."

In deepest night his mother sent her son forth.
Ah, that mother who did not cling to her son:
   mighty cliff!

The kingdom was founded in the land of Cholbon beside
   the Piryu River.

If you are sons of this land, I say:
"Sons!
Go and speak in the tongue of your kingdom.
Free yourselves of your fathers.
Free yourselves of your fathers,
and free yourselves of your fathers' names.
Make your own names."

Grandmother

Cow eyes
those dull vacant eyes
my grandmother's eyes.

My grandmother!
The most sacred person in the world to me.

A cow that has stopped grazing the fresh grass
and is just standing there.

But she's not my grandmother after all:
rather, this world's peace,

dead and denied a tomb.

Lee Dong-hui's Wits*

Night and day, his only thought was our people's good.
He was a tall man.
Arriving in Kando he administered Kwangsŏng
    Middle School,
but finding himself with a ton of debts, he lived by his wits
and vanished from sight.
He sent the lad Song Ch'ang-kŭn to his compatriots
with a letter apparently from bandits, saying:
"Put a ransom in the cave at such a place
by such a day and such a time.
Otherwise, we will kill your Chosŏn General
    Lee Dong-hui."
After sending out that letter
he went to the cave at such a place
on such a day at such a time
but found no sign of money or of people.
At which he climbed to the top of Soyŏngja Rock
in Kando's Hualien Province,
and there he lamented:

"Everybody cares only for themselves,
forgetful of the nation. Oh, what shall we do?"
After which he went to Kabarovsk in East Siberia,
renounced his education, and started to fight.

Ch'ŏl-gon from Okjŏng-gol

In Okjŏng-gol Valley,
or over the hill in Yongtol-ri,
or outside the West Gate,
as Ch'ŏl-gon wandered furtively about,
people would mock: "That idiot's wandering about again."
Yet paying no heed to this or that,
he'd always be laughing,
laughing even on nights bright with gourd-flowers.
There was just one day without any laughter,
the day Kil-mo's father was whipped almost to death
by the Japanese policeman.

New Year's Full Moon*

Bitter cold day, the new year's first full moon,
a special day.
One housewife, busy from early morning,
knowing that beggars will be coming by,
puts out a pot of five-grain rice in anticipation
on the stone mortar
that stands beside her brush-wood gate,
with a single side-dish of plantain-shoots.
Soon, an ancient beggar comes breezing up,
makes ready to spin a yarn but finally
just pockets the rice and goes on his way.
If only we had 360 more days like today in a year!
His bag is soon bulging.
His round complete, as he's leaving the village
he runs into another beggar:
glad encounter!
You've no call to go there, I've done 'em all!
Let's us celebrate a Fool Moon too!

Snapping dried twigs, they make a fire
to thaw themselves by, then
producing hunks of rice from this house and that,
the two beggars set to,
choking, laughing with mouths full.
Soon bands of magpies hear the news
and flock flapping about.

Chŏng Yong-gi of the Righteous Army

At the age of a flower he died like a flower.
Young Chŏng Yong-gi of the Righteous Army died
   in battle.
At which his aged father Chŏng Hwan-jik set off
and hurried to the battlefield where his son had died.
When the battle was over he was caught by the Japs.
This is the song he left behind at dawn on his
   execution day:
"Even though they kill me, my heart will never change.
Righteousness is a heavy thing, while death is
   something light.
Who can I ask to look after my affairs?
The more I think about it, the more I see a bright dawn
   is here."

The Wife from Suregi*

At Frog Embankment
there are only frogs, all the rest of the world is dead.
The wife from Suregi is weeping there,
but the croaking of frogs drowns out her weeping.
This evening is the tenth anniversary of her
    husband's death.
She's managed to get some barley to cook, digs spoon
    and chopsticks
into the bowl in ritual offering, and weeps.
Her metal spoon and chopsticks are gone, taken by
    the Japs.
Digging a wooden spoon and chopsticks into the bowl,
    she weeps.
At Frog Embankment
she weeps but the croaking of frogs drowns out
    her weeping.
It's no use to her dead husband's ears.

Old Foster Father

See that migrant lapwing perching on a branch!
There was an old man used to say birds weren't
    strangers either.
Even when he was upset
he would never go on and on bitterly complaining,
although his cuffs were caked with dirt.
And his sons, the apples of his eye,
he lost them both:
one died of cholera,
the other fell into the water and drowned.
He could barely sigh. He had nothing to live for.
Then, once past forty,
he began collecting foster children, one after another.
There was one was about ten years old.
Another who had lost both parents early on.
He took them all into his house,
made them his own, then sent them out at the
    proper time.
When harvest festival season came
unkind neighbors used to make sly remarks about
why does a man need so many foster children?

While to each the old man would dole out a measure
of fresh jujubes he had beaten from the tree
and simply answer in a quiet level voice:
"If only you realized how precious people are!
Isn't each person like a parent or a child?"
And when that old man had done weeding
between the rows in his hillside bean-patch,
as he watched how the sluggish uphill-climbing breeze
overturned the bean-leaves with a flash of white,
he would mutter: "Here, it's that rogue's
    birthday tomorrow,
better pop a middling hen in a bag presently
and call in there on the way back home.
He's a growing lad: not good if he's hungry, not good
    at all."

Il-man's Father

The sea off the west coast isn't quite a real sea.
It's more like some nearby neighbor
clearing his throat, like a neighbor's house,
like the yard of a neighbor's house
on a sultry day
where the smell of smoke lingers even after the fire's out.

Surely no one could ever return from such a sea.

It's been five years since Il-man's father
    from Paekdang-mei
went off as a seaman thanks to people he knew.
He spent five years on boats catching shrimp
    and whitebait
out near Kaeya Island.

Il-man's father used to spit on his hands
and handle rope so deftly,
a ribbon bound tightly round his head.
Now Il-man's grown up,
he's the spitting image of his father.
Il-man is Il-man's father.

Daughter

Old Nam-su used to be good at hunting hares.
Two days after he died,
Ok-sun, his married daughter,
followed the road out of the village for a mile,
hair dishevelled, weeping like she was about to die.
She wept blindly, blinded by tears,
then once she arrived back in the village
all the women emerged from one house after another,
clicked their tongues,
then they all began to lament with her
until the whole village was full of grief.
Now the dead man can lie in peace, satisfied.
Yes indeed,
it's good to have fruitful years, even for grief.

The Wife from Kaesari

Although she brought up three sons
as stout as big fat toads,
the wife from Kaesari never so much as once
coughed out loud after getting married.
No matter what anyone said,
her only reply was a reluctant *mmm*
and even that didn't really leave her lips,
a tiny sound, eager to quickly crawl back in again.
Among the neighborhood women
no one had ever been seen with such a tiny voice
as the wife from Kaesari.
Once her eldest son was married,
she never spoke harshly
to her daughter-in-law
but merely stitched away at a torn hemp jacket.
She took care that no one heard the sound
of her blowing out the kerosene lamps.
The wife from Kaesari
went into a decline in her last year of life.
No one knew just what was wrong with her.
When she was dying, her three sons were in her room
waiting for the end to come.

Knowing no eloquence in her lifetime,
she was incapable of any decent last words.
She was more or less heard to say
the lid of the soy-sauce jar up on the terrace
ought to be opened to the daylight
and also, it seems,
that the lining in father's jacket ought to be replaced.
Then in a flash she expired.

Chae-hak's Finger

Dad's closest friend, Chae-hak, always reliable,
and Uncle Kyŏng-sŏp, and Dad, were three
   sworn brothers.
After ten years had passed and Uncle Kyŏng-sŏp
was already dead, when Kyŏng-sŏp's father was lying sick,
Chae-hak cut off a finger in place of his dead son
and fed him his blood as a remedy.
When Chae-hak used to come to visit our home,
while still far off he would start to repeat:
"Big Brother, Big Brother!" Then Dad,
who might be treading chopped straw mixed with clay
to replaster a wall, would go dashing out,
feet muddy, happily exclaiming:
"*Ho ho*, Little Brother's on his way!"
Chae-hak's special talent for making liquor
was well-known throughout Kunsan and Okgu,
where every brewery was eager to have him
but he wouldn't budge, refused to quit
the backroom of the Mijei brewery:
"If I go far away, we blood brothers will be parted.
I'll not leave, no, never."

Even without one finger,
if he swirled the mix with his hand as he made it,
	the savor
of that *makkŏlli* or hooch would cleave to the weary palate.
When a load of three or four gallons of *makkŏlli* went off
	to some farm,
he'd stand watching with folded arms as if seeing off his
	own child
for he had no children but the liquor served instead.
One evening when it was raining fit to drown the world,
Chae-hak arrived exclaiming: 'Big Brother, Big Brother!
I won't make liquor any more.
After someone drank my liquor, blood was shed.
Hong Sŏng-dŏk from Wŏndang-ri's dead, stabbed by
	Pak Kwan-su.
After drinking, they started to fight about
	irrigation rights…"

Uncle Maeng-sik

Someone like watered wine,
so insipid he even bows down before kids.
As taseless as insipid *makkŏlli*,
but so erudite,
he knows all there is to be known.
Someone who comes home from the rice fields at nightfall
riding on an ox
but knows about more than just oxen.
Ah, the void! *Ah*, the dread
of days when snow is billowing down,
days when snow is filling every corner of the world.
Yet uncle simply throws open the front gate and exclaims:
"*Ah-ha*, it's really snowing!
I wonder: how will all the wild animals survive?"

Hyegong: A Monk in the Days of Old*

Under the system of slavery to be found in Silla society
there might be three thousand slaves in the household
of certain eminent ruling families
who not uncommonly had fierce private armies too.
Even respectable citizens were reduced to slavery
by their rulers' practice of grain-hoarding.
Born the child of one such slave,
the Venerable Hyegong
successfully escaped
and became a monk in a temple of poor reputation,
roaming about with a straw basket turned over on
    his head,
roaming up and down all over Silla.
Although he was a monk, he never once put on
    silken robes
and when he was famished
in the course of his roaming, he'd catch a fish
in some shallow streamlet,
chew it up raw and still flapping:
"*Ah!* I'm full.
Ah! Buddha's full."

Then he'd piss and his piss
would bring the fish he'd eaten back to life
and it would go swimming off down the streamlet again,
or so people said.
The Buddhist monks of Silla days
had reduced the nation from riches to rags
but the Venerable Hyegong had only rags.
How will you lead
the world all alone?
As for Wŏnhyo, he too danced the dance
of no boundaries as he went along.
How can the world be put right?
Monks,
if you intend to reform the world,
if you hope to stroll about the Pure Land,
join together.
The grass that grows in sun and rain
is made stronger by the blowing wind.
Join together.
Unite in the sight of the sun.

No-More's Mother*

Three daughters had already been born
to No-More's parents over in Kalmoe:
Tŏk-sun,
        Bok-sun,
                Kil-sun.
Then another daughter emerged. Once again
the sacred straw stretching across the gate
held bits of charcoal, but no red peppers!
She got the name "No-More."
Furious, No-More's father went drinking.
When he came home, he declared:
"A woman that can only have girls
deserves to be kicked out of the house!"
He grabbed his wife by the hair,
although she'd not yet fully recovered,
and dragged her outside,
smashing down the rotten fence.
"Uhuhuh!" he cried. A fine sight.
But oh the tasty red-pepper paste
that No-More's mother makes!

How does she do it? Why, people come
from Namwŏn—Sunch'ang, even—
eager to learn the art of her pepper-paste.
A few of the myriad pepper-red dragonflies
that fill the clear, late-autumn skies
often fly down and perch on the heavy lids
of the pots bulging with red-pepper paste
up on the frugal storage platform
there behind the house.
The local women at the well,
with much smacking of lips, claim
this special pepper paste is made
by No-More's mother and the red dragonflies,
working together, a collaboration!
On one such day, Sun-ch'ŏl's ma came sneaking
into the bamboo-fenced back yard
to scoop out a bowl of the famous paste,
and it just so happened Tŏk-sun was there,
washing her back.
Struck by the sight of that abundant flesh
she murmured:
"My! Sun-ch'ŏl, dear, it's Tŏk-sun here
that you should marry! A hometown bride!
I never saw such a luscious girl!"

The Women from Sŏnjei-ri

In darkest night, near midnight, the dogs
in the middle of Saet'ŏ begin their raucous barking.
One dog barks, so the next one barks
until the dogs at Kalmoe across the fields
follow suit and start to bark as well.
Between the barking of dogs,
scraps of voices echo: *eh ah oh* …
Not unlike the sound which the night's wild geese
let fall upon the bitter cold ground
as they fly over, high above,
not unlike that splendid sound
echoing back and forth.
It's women from Sŏnjei-ri on their way home
from the old-style market over at Kunsan
where they'd gone with garlic bulbs by the hundreds
in baskets on their heads,
there being a shortage of *kimch'i* cabbages
from the bean-fields.

Now they're on their way home,
after getting rid of what couldn't be sold
at the clearing auction at closing time —
several miles gone,
several miles left to go in deepest night!
The empty baskets may be light enough
yet I wonder: just how light are they
with empty stomachs, nothing to eat?
Still, they don't suffer alone.
They share this pain,
these plain, simple people,
these plain, simple women.
What a good homely life!
Perhaps the dogs have gotten used to their voices,
for the barking starts to die away.
Night seems eager to declare: "I myself am night!"
And the darkness blinks its vacant eyes.

Volume 2 (1986)

A Dead Dog

On digging up the heating flue under the floor
when it refused to draw properly,
we found a dog that had disappeared from the house.
It was dead, of course.
Cautiously, Father took it up into the hill behind the
  house and buried it.
The next day it rained. As the rain made the leaves
green again, they barked.

Pyŏng-ok

If you're born a yokel out in the backwoods
once you've reached five or six
there's no time left for play,
forced to become a drudge
following your father,
with work piling up like the hills.
When autumn comes
if mother tells you to bring home mud-snails
you go rushing out to the rice-paddy:
foraging for snails half a day
in the wide open spaces out there
is great, really great.
Being away from his rotten job is great.
Pyŏng-ok,
expert snail-catcher Pyŏng-ok,
drank lye by mistake and died.
None of the neighborhood kids know
where he's buried.
If a kid dies there's no tomb, no offerings:
there'll be another one born by-and-by.

Pong-t'ae

You and I vied for first place in grade-school.
You from a rich house
had really nice clothes
your five buttons always shining bright and
every day a boiled egg snuggled
bright in your lunch-box, where the white rice
contained very little barley
but you were never boastful, oh no,
not by so much as a fingernail-paring.
We had a paddy-field just beside yours.
"Let's you and I get on well together,"
you said, and gave me dried rice-cakes.
But Pong-t'ae
first your father died
when the Reds pulled back north
then you were dragged off by the local people
died in a cave in Halmi Mountain
shot by a black UN soldier.
One moonlit night
in a dark cave you died.

Pong-t'ae, *ah!*
I couldn't do anything to save you,
though you were sixteen
and I was sixteen.

Chae-suk

Chae-suk, the girl from the house by the well,
a brimming crock of water perched on her head,
gazes into the far-off distance as she walks along.
The early autumn open road lies clear ahead.
Next year
Chae-suk will be leaving here.
Chae-suk's heart swells in expectation.
Chae-suk, so like the darkness left after the moon's
    gone down

The Well*

There's a well in the yard of that house,
a well more than ten fathoms deep.
In Pullye's snug family house,
Pullye's mother, bright as a gourd-flower,
and little Pullye, a lily-flower,
live together, just the two of them.
The mother a widow, young,
discreet in every word,
never dousing herself with water,
even in midsummer heat.
When I used to go on errands there,
if I took one sip of the blue-black water,
of that water's silence and the dread
that Pullye's mother,
letting down the heavy bucket,
drew up from her ten-fathom well,
my whole body would tremble, my heart would pound.

Tip-Taker Mun

Tip-taker Mun lives in the first
of the three small villages comprising Kaesa-ri.
In every gambling house and at every card-table
on the straw mats spread at every wake
and at every friendly match,
not just sometimes here and there
but invariably, he turns up,
just like the blowfly that turns up, *bzzz,*
the minute you squat bare-bottomed up some hill.
He yawns his way through the night
an unwelcome guest
finally receiving a penny tip from each of the big winners
that he carefully collects, then goes home
and tells his wife:
"No luck last night,
here's all I won."
To which his wife replies:
"If my husband tip-taker Mun gets this much, it's fine."

Man-sun*

Her face was a mass of freckles,
as if she'd been liberally sprinkled with sesame seed,
but her brows were fine, and her eyes so lovely
they made breezes spring up from the hills and plains.
Her shadow falling across the water
was like nothing else in this world.
Near the end of Japanese rule, after she had picked
and handed in the castor beans,
she left, wearing a headband stamped with the
    Japanese flag,
to become a comfort woman.
A woman from the Mijei Patriotic Wives Union took
    her away,
saying she was off to earn money at a factory
making airplane tails.
Took her away with the Japanese flag flying.
Then, *ho-ho*, a bottle of liquor
and a ration ticket for rice arrived at her family's house
from the village captain.
"*Ho-ho*, what have we done to deserve such a favor?"

After Liberation, when everyone came back
not a word was heard from Man-sun...
though white campanulas blossomed
and cicadas sang.

The Two Pok-dongs of Mijei

In Mijei village you have Kim Pok-dong
and you also have Hong Pok-dong.
With just a few years difference between them,
it's a close enough relationship,
except they're fighting all the time,
enough to live up to their twin names,
fighting, if you can call it fighting,
but not using their fists, merely
grabbing each other by the throat and squeezing,
putting everything into that one throttling hand
just growling,
just breathing hard.
The neighbors out to view the fight find it dull,
like watching dogs mate,
like watching snakes tangle:
"Oh dear! the Pok-dongs are fighting again.
Better go and fetch some rock salt
to add some flavor to some dull fighting."

Kim Ch'ang-suk*

From the very beginning he was on to
Syngman Rhee and all his wicked tricks.
In the days of the Shanghai Provisional Government
he hated Syngman Rhee's games and fought against him.
Their fight lost none of its force with the years
and in 1950 he was dismissed from his post
as head of the main Confucian Shrine.

Long years passed
sixteen years in prison
legs crippled by torture
long enough for him never to walk again.

Five hundred years of effort were not wasted
producing one man worthy
of the Confucian ethics of Chosŏn times.

He had a true man's tears
a true man's wrath
a manly, bitter spirit.

He used to declare:
"See those pseudo-soldiers over there?
Well, they'll soon be swept from this land,
and if I die in battle, I'll have no regrets."

The Twins' Mother

Pyŏng-hyŏn and Pyŏng-jin's mother?
Look at her, bare breasts dangling,
as she rushes around in all directions.
After the monsoons have demolished the outhouse,
not caring if the menfolk see or not,
she bares her bottom in the millet-crunchy fields
and pisses freely. That kind of woman.
If there's nothing to eat at home,
she grubs up a neighbor's greens to cook.
What a woman! If one of the twins
comes running home screaming
from being punched playing with the local kids:
"A pox on you! May lightning strike you dead!
No one would think you were born
on fresh straw one midsummer dog-day!
How come you get beaten up all the time?"
That's how wild the twins' mother is
and yet even such a woman must once have known
shy modest days of maidenhood,
those very very precious days!

Ch'ung-jo, My Little Brother

At the end of the Japanese period we had nothing to eat.
There were no trees on the hills.
Springtime was dreary without azaleas.
Ch'ung-jo, my little brother,
born when I was already a big boy,
chose that wretched time to come into the world.
Mother was carted off on a wagon down Shiorit road
to the hospital near the harbor.
A rough tampon inserted
to keep his head from popping out,
she was carted off on a rickety wagon;
he kept trying to be born but the passage was blocked
as mother hung on to the wagon side
and screamed bloody murder.
So they went off
down Shiorit road
and the kid was born in a hospital called
Guam Hospital so we called him the Guam Kid:
that's how Ch'ung-jo my little brother was born.
Once out, he grew up fine.
He'd go racing off, a pinwheel in his hand.

My brother lived through
Independence, the War, the 1960 Revolution
then just past thirty he died of leukemia.
That kid could work up the beat of any old song,
merrily singing and dancing.

Uncle Yong-sul*

Uncle Yong-sul went to Changch'un up in Manchuria.
and to Bongch'ŏn too, where
he was said to have lived with a Russian woman.
Uncle Yong-sul was said to have ridden around
in a carriage and pair…
Not a bit of it.
He came back with nothing to call his own but himself,
wrinkles creeping across his forehead.
He came back hollow cheeked, chin and
    bones protruding.
But uncle's voice
was just the same as before,
so when he exclaimed: "My, you look well!"
things past all became new
at that voice of his, that familiar voice,
when it rang out anew,
newer than fresh grass in springtime or
    sprouting mugwort.

Earthworm

Once you're six you count stars.
Evenings are great,
daytimes are bad.
With Mother out in the fields,
Father out in the rice-paddies,
in other folk's rice-paddies,
in the daytime,
once a shower has passed,
you play with earthworms beneath the eaves.

So does one six-year-old, known as Idle Do-sŏp, wait
for evening.

Six-Fingers

At thirty, Six-Fingers is still unmarried.
He has one finger too many
to do more and more work.
Yet his right hand is always generous.
It's inborn,
nothing to be awkward about, not much, at least.
With that hand
Six-Fingers can weave mesh bags very well
and plait fine bush-clover baskets.
With both legs stretched out,
running through a folksong tune to get started,
weaving big round straw mats,
he just keeps on sitting quietly,
no matter how upside-down the world gets turned,
and if some troublesome fellow comes creeping up
and tries to surprise him with a sudden noise,
he just keeps on quietly weaving straw mats,
saying: "There's no way you can frighten me
Come here,
        eat this,"
offering him with his eyes a cold sweet potato,
boiled yesterday.

Solemnly, Chae-bong's father says:
"That Six-Fingers has the very soul of a Buddha,
right here in town."
That's what he says, at least, but do you think
he's ready to let him marry one of his two daughters?
That's quite absurd, of course.
How ever could he?
Bumper crops and Buddhas are nothing but words.

Ŭisang, the Great Monk

Born of Silla aristocracy,
he became a monk at twenty. At thirty
he served the great master Wŏnhyo like a brother.
Because Wŏnhyo did not like the sea all that much
when Wŏnhyo and Ŭisang decided to visit T'ang China
they set out overland through the realm of Koguryŏ.
But they were arrested on suspicion of spying for Silla,
after which they went back home, to Silla.
The next time, they set out to go by sea
from the port of Tangjin, in the realm of Paekje.
Arriving at the port,
Ŭisang crossed the sea alone,
Wŏnhyo no longer seeing any reason to visit China:
in pitch black night, he'd drunk water from a skull
then gone back home the next morning
having understood that "Mind makes all things."
Ŭisang liked the sea very much.
That explains why later, after his return,
he lived at Naksan Temple beside the East Sea.
Ŭisang and Shan-miao, a Chinese girl from Tung-ju,
    fell in love.

That Chinese girl
made Ŭisang's clothes and supplied his needs.
At Ch'ing-ch'an Temple in the Chungnan Mountains,
    he became
a pupil of Chih-yen the great Hua-yen master
then after being recognized by Chih-yen and Tao-hsuan,
became their main disciple, together with
    Fa-tsang Hsien-shou.
Ŭisang's chanting of the Garland Sutra was
    magnificent, marvelous.
He had only to chant it
and people would exclaim:
"The mind is full! The cosmos is replete! The Dharma
    is replete!"
But perhaps because the Hua-yen was limited in China to
    the elite,
it was utter mumbo-jumbo to ordinary people.
When China had laid waste the realms of Paekje
    and Koguryŏ
and was on the verge of laying waste to Silla too,
Hua-yen master Ŭisang hurried home.
He came home alone, without his dear love, Shan-miao.
Once back home,
he did not enter the high society of Silla
but took to the solitude of the East Sea.

Intending to teach Hua-yen far and wide,
he thought of founding a temple
in Yŏngju below Sobaek Mountain,
but then Shan-miao, who had crossed the seas in quest of
    her love,
brought him a stone
and he founded his temple on that floating stone.
Preserved among the treasures at Kouzanji Temple
    in Japan
is a painting of the founder of the Hua-yen School, where
the love of Ŭisang and the beautiful Shan-miao has
    been preserved;
and, *ah*, just try reading Ŭisang's *Songs of Samadhi*:
they're marvelous, truly marvelous!
A whole lifetime with nothing but one set of clothing,
one bottle, one rice bowl —
the fields and slaves that King Munmu gave him, all
    sent back:
"Our Buddhist faith affirms equality, no high nor low,
for that does not correspond to human mortality.
How could I have slaves or accumulate wealth?
What would be the use? What use?
As a monk, all of Buddha Land is my house,
and, owning just one rice-bowl, I live on what I farm.

Building a fortress with iron tools
would not end suffering."
The chill moonlight on cold late autumn evenings!
The unwavering gaze of Ŭisang in that chill!

Widow Paek from Hamdŏk-ri

Kim Ki-ho, a boatman from Hamdŏk-ri in Cheju Island
together with his uncle Chong-hŭng
set out in a fishing boat.
They encountered a storm. The boat overturned.
They never returned.
His wife, Paek by name,
called out her friends the diving-women   .
and they began to look for her husband's body,
searching for eight days all over the open sea
in vain.
They called upon a monk and offered prayers to
   the Dragon King,
in vain.
His wife, made a widow at only twenty-five,
purified herself,
then plunged into the sea,
down deep into the sea,
and recovered the corpse of her husband Kim Ki-ho
jammed underwater between some rocks,
or what was left of it after the fishes had done nibbling.
Holding it in her arms, she broke the surface.

Then
without taking time to weep,
without grieving,
taking the remains of the corpse,
she wrapped it in a shroud,
laid it in a pine coffin,
and, lo!, held the funeral at the top of
    their field.
Every morning standing in front of his grave,
she informed him about this and that to be done that day.
In the evening she would go and give a detailed report
as to what had been done or could not be done that day,
then went back home
to feed her only son,
fed him on fresh laver soup too,
lived light-heartedly serving him instead of a husband.
In the evenings when spring tides rose high,
facing the black sea spray as it rose above the land,
she listened to her husband's voice,
the sound of waves.

Tomb of Tools

The sea flooded the salt ponds of the Mankyŏng River
and Su-kil
who used to play the drum so well,
out gathering salt
in the midst of that maelstrom,
was swept away in the flood.
They never found so much as a shoe
let alone his corpse.
Su-kil's brothers
and his married sisters
debated
then decided to build him a cenotaph
in which they laid
the tools Su-kil had used:
with all their handles removed,
hoe, mattock, spade, and rake.
So he was buried in the ancestral cemetery.
A tomb of tools it was.
For some reason the village kids never went near
    that tomb.

For some reason that empty tomb was frightening.
But three years later,
lo and behold, Su-kil came back, alive.
His brothers at first recoiled in horror,
thinking it was a ghost.
Only after Su-kil had shouted out several times:
"I'm not a ghost, I'm not,"
they embraced him
and wept, exclaiming: "It's a dream, he's alive!"
Swept away in the flood,
far out at sea
he came across a plank,
a narrow escape if ever there was one,
and was swept down to the sea off Ch'ilsan
where he came across a boat
where the sailors declared:
"In return for saving your life, you must serve us a while."
For the next three years he cooked the meals in the boat
and he escaped at last at Popsang-p'o and came
    home alive.
Su-kil dug up the tomb,
retrieved his tools,

fitted them out with new handles,
stuck one into the ground and said:
"You're alive, and I'm alive, and
as ever, there's a lot of work to be done."

Real Penny-Pinchers

In the days of King Ch'ŏlchong in the Chosŏn Era
there was a man by the name of Kim Penny-Pincher,
who lived in the Changdan region, near Seoul.
One day he sent his son to the house of
    Chang Penny-Pincher
to borrow a hammer.
His son returned empty-handed.
"They won't lend it. They said we'd wear it out
    hammering nails."
Hearing that, Kim Penny-Pincher growled:
"Ah, that scoundrel's a real penny-pincher.
Well, there's nothing we can do. Bring me our hammer.
It's in the left-hand recess of the cupboard in my room.
It's a hammer handed down from your
    great-great-grandfather."
Now, if you go beyond Changdan,
you'll find the Kaesŏng Penny-Pincher,
and farther still the Haeju Penny-Pincher.

It seems the Kaesŏng Penny-Pincher
used to water down his urine before selling it for manure,
while the Haeju Penny-Pincher,
when buying urine,
used to dip in a finger and taste it first,
to see if had been watered down or not.
It was by penny-pinchers like these
that commerce was first established in Chosŏn times.
Nowadays such penny-pinchers are nowhere to be seen
and the nation is in a sorry state.
In that case, surely,
penny-pinchers are vital. They're the essence of
    our people.

Plum Blossom

The house in Saet'ŏ where Omok lives
is only a tiny thatched cottage and yet
so spick and span,
lacking in nothing, be it
rice, barley, wheat, soy-beans, red-beans, maize,
sorghum, millet, or oats,
all the traditional five or seven kinds of grain and corn,
all there:
the most frugal household around.
Omok's mother:
such a careful housekeeper
with her hair tidy in a bun,
her apron never off.
When she winnows the rice,
sesame, or millet, not one stray seed
escapes from the tossing.
Beside that house,
when winter is gone
and spring returns,
two plum trees
stand blooming,

so although the house is empty
when the two are out working in the fields,
those trees make the house all brightness.

One fine day or other some lucky fellow
will come courting
and carry off Omok, so like her mother.
He'll carry her off on his back,
on his back. I hope he gets sore feet.

Volume 3 (1986)

The Ditch

Go and look in the drainage ditch.
The water there is so friendly, you say,
like an old lady.
Like a matronly lady
who's weathered her fair share of hardships.
Well, it's all lies!
Chaenam's little maid,
running errands along that far-off ditch,
fell in and drowned.
A child without a name,
without parents.
All the time everywhere her master's eye watching,
she had no place to cry alone,
that child could never properly cry.
Go and look in the ditch.
It's like that child.
The water that drowned that child
is like that child.

Hey, You There!

Setting to work
long before the dawn chorus begins,
and only stopping at midnight
when the evening star is setting:
housework knows no glory, no end.
Field-work, now, or paddyfield-work,
they have an end, but
for the maid of old Hankyu's concubine
there's no glory, no end.
A house with mountains of meals to prepare
and tables of drinks to serve.
Just look at that girl, the sixth to go there:
can it already be two years ago?
It was the year of the great famine
so she thought herself lucky
to survive on left-over scraps from meals.
If she hears someone call: Hey, you there!
even though she's working round back,
she replies: Right away!

and comes running out to the yard in front,
or maybe she's beside the pump,
rinsing the washing in lye,
or wringing out a pile of washing
bigger than herself, but
if she hears someone call: Hey, you there!
she replies: Right away!
and hurries to where her mistress is.
From time to time local women say:
Still can't you see? In another year's time
you'll be all knocked to bits!
Go somewhere else to find your meals,
else you'll land one that'll be the end of you!
But in one ear and out the other. Look:
lowering a bucket into the well
at the end of that rope that must weigh a ton,
she nearly went down with the rope into the well!
Hey, you there!
                         Hey, you there!

Poor Wretch

Old Pak Ch'ŏn-bong in Kalmei is really stingy.
If some kids have got hold of just one barley cake,
he wheedles it slyly from them and eats it himself.
You think that's all?
He goes into houses secretly,
steals the nightsoil from the cesspit
and puts it on his field.
Then all his vegetables suddenly shrivel and die
on contact with so much over-rich manure.
If there's an irrigation dispute,
old Ch'ŏn-bong's always involved.
If he goes to work for someone,
he works half a day, says he's sick, and leaves.
A few days later he insists he worked all day
and gets paid in full.
If he attends the rites at a house in mourning,
once the funeral's over he insists on being paid for that.
He may be past fifty,
it's the same as when he was a kid.
Call as you like: "Ch'ŏn-bong-a, Ch'ŏn-bong-a!"

he ignores adults like you
and goes off to where infants of five or six are playing,
wheedles the bags of marbles from their
    waistcoat pockets,
plays against them, wins all the marbles,
then sells them back to the kids
and earns himself a few small coins.
When other old men can't afford to eat or wear clothes
they collapse and die in droves.
Old miser Ch'ŏn-bong's face
shines out ruddier than ever
without a trace of shame.
He's the only really strong one around,
never catches a cold at seasons' turn,
always hale and hearty.
And it's not only him.
There's his wife too.
She borrows people's things
and if you aren't very careful,
those things become hers.
"What, I borrowed the cotton gin from your house?
Why, it's ours.
It's ours."

The Little Spring

Without its little spring,
what would make Yongtun Village a village?
Endlessly, snowflakes fall
into the spring's dark waters
and dissolve.
What still still stillness,
as Yang-sul's wife,
covered in snow, goes out to draw water,
puts down her tiny little water jar
and picks up the gourd dipper but forgets to draw water,
watching snowflakes die:
that still still stillness.

Wu-yŏl's Family House in Wuittŭm

The house at the back of Pong-t'ae's
belongs to Ko Wu-yŏl.
Did you see that house's pigsty?
Why! you might go all over Korea
and not find one as clean as that,
so clean that if you dropped some food,
not for pigs but for people,
they'd eat it straight off the floor.
Clean enough to make offerings
for honored ancestors.
Ko Wu-yŏl's father?
Diligent as a new moon,
not a single weed growing anywhere,
not a single cobweb.
What's more, Wu-yŏl's mother
keeps everything so tidy indoors and out
that when the flies come swarming inside
with the first winter frosts,
you'll never find more than a few in their house.
And look at that house's sewage outlet!
Is that a drain, or a clear mountain stream?

In other houses, when they spread newly harvested millet
    to dry,
it's laid on the ground all mixed with leaves and dust,
but in that house's yard a good straw mat
holds it to welcome the sun's visitation.
Wu-yŏl
with his younger sister,
each seizing an old broom,
clean everything spick-and-span before breakfast.
But —
no one ever goes to that house
in the hope of borrowing even a handful of barley or rice.
And around back a lonesome pomegranate ripens.

The Table Seller

Once or twice every year
the table seller visits our village.
The winnowing basket seller's a woman but
the table seller has to carry ten or twelve
tables about so of course
it's got to be a man,
a man with a face like a brigand,
a man with a straggly beard.
"Buy my tables! Buy my tables!"
Local women
and table seller
are bound to talk together.
He goes round all the villages
yet still feels awkward towards women,
so while his lips are talking
his eyes look somewhere else.
The local women
are used to their husbands and the other local menfolk
but when they meet the table seller
and bargain with him over the price,
somehow

they loose all interest in buying a new table,
they playfully tease the seller instead.
"Why, if you're all the time off visiting far away places,
what becomes of the woman you've left at home?
What fun is there for her?"
The table seller replies awkwardly:
"That woman's water laced with water,
it's alright."
"Alright? How can it be alright?"
Oh yes, it's alright
to chatter like this with an unknown man.

Spirit Shrine

We pray for a safe journey
by throwing a stone at the spirit shrine.
That wasn't something I learned from Dad
but by the time I was three I was already throwing stones.
Throwing a stone at the spirit shrine,
we pray that things go badly for those we hate.
We pray they suffer loss.
But we do not pray for the death of those we hate.
Farmers' old-style curses
extend only so far.
No matter how wretched they may be
their curses extend only so far.
But near the end of the Japanese Era
when stomachs were empty
and people were beside themselves,
very often a stone was thrown
and people went so far as to pray:
"May the kids of rich So-and-So die.
May rich So-and-So's father neither live long nor rest
    in peace."
The pile of stones at the spirit shrine kept growing higher.

The wife of Pak Tae-gon
told the rich people in the big house
about such prayers
and the rascal Su-dong who'd said such a prayer
was summoned to the yard of the house of rich
    Kaneoka
where he got beaten with clubs
by the household serfs
and the owner's oldest, Kaneoka Taro.
Soon after that, the rascal Su-dong
threw a stone late at night at the house of rich
    Kaneoka.
Instead of the spirit shrine,
instead of throwing a stone then praying,
in the guise of a ghost
he threw stones at the paper covering the door
of the owner's bedroom.
He was at once put in the police-station cell.
He did a month inside
then he came out.
He kept crying.
The dogs barked.

Sang-p'il and His Brother

Their father had been dead ten years
when relations soured between Sang-p'il and Sang-gu,
who used to get on so well.
Inevitably, they began by cultivating
the upper and lower rice fields separately;
then there was a flood
and they fought over water.
Now with farming folk, fights over water are common
    dog fights
but to see the fight between those brothers with rolled
    up sleeves,
everyone in the whole village turned out.
Hong-sik pulled them apart:
"What kind of disrespectful behavior do you call this,
in full sight of your father's grave up there?"
After that,
on the ninth day of the eleventh month, their
    father's anniversary,
they each made offerings in their own house.
When the elder brother Sang-p'il
heard that Sang-gu was making offerings separately,
he went rushing across

and kicked the table over.

"You scoundrel! How can a spirit receive offerings in two
   different houses?"

At that Sang-gu and his wife exclaimed:

"Why, father

has renounced his elder son, he's not worth half a dime,

he's got no son but me!"

Cleaning up the overturned offering-table,

Sang-gu's wife is weeping bitterly. Pitiful!

Wangsanak*

When he plucked the strings of his *kŏmungo*,
a black crane would come flying down and dance to it.
Koguryŏ was a nation of warriors, yet there
a *kŏmungo*, player became prime minister.
The prime minister in the days of King Kwanggaet'o
used to rule this vast land
by the sound of his *kŏmungo*.
He composed a hundred tunes
and as the nation prospered the *kŏmungo*, prospered.
It was exported to China
and to Paekche in the south,
as well as to Japan across the sea.
Still dancing, the black crane followed the sound,
    they say.
In the north, Wangsanak
in the south, Wurŭk.
Their sounds have served this land, sounds alive and dead.

The Hunter of Kaema Heights

In the days after King Sejong conquered the
    northern frontier,
when Im P'an-gŏl the Hairy Hunter of Kaema Heights
    went hunting,
he came home each time with just one beast.
He was a demon at hunting.
The wild boars smelt him with their fine noses and fled.
But they knew that if they all fled,
the Hairy Hunter would get raging mad
and catch as many as he could,
so the canny boars took counsel together
and one always stayed behind as prey for the hunter.
Only
that meant that the outcome of hairy Im P'ang-gŏl's
    hunting
had nothing to do with his skill, it was all
by courtesy of the boars.
But at last Im P'an-gŏl
fell down in some hunting ground
and all the boars of Kaema Heights came dashing out
    at once:
"The moment has come!

The moment we've been waiting for!
You get the head,
you get an arm,
you get a thigh,
you get the trunk,
you get his balls."
They shared him out and gobbled him up,
then scattered over the snow-covered slopes.
And that was it!

Headmaster Abe

Headmaster Abe Sudomu from Japan
with his round glasses: a fearsome man,
fiery-hot like the spiciest peppers.
When he clacked down the hallway
in slippers cut from a pair of old boots,
he cast a deathly hush over every class.
In my second year during ethics class
he asked us what we hoped to become.
Kids replied:
"I want to be a general in the Imperial Army!"
"I want to become an admiral!"
"I want to become another Yamamoto Isoroko!"
"I want to become a nursing orderly!"
"I want to become a mechanic in a plane factory
and make planes to defeat the American and
    British devils!"
Then Headmaster Abe asked me to reply.
I leaped to my feet:
"I want to become the Emperor!"
No sooner were those words spoken
than a thunderbolt fell from the blue:
"You have formally blasphemed the venerable name

of his Imperial Majesty: you are expelled this instant!"
On hearing that, I collapsed into my seat.
But the class master pleaded,
my father put on clean clothes and came and pleaded,
and by the skin of my teeth, instead of being expelled,
I was punished by being sent to spend a few months
sorting through a stack of rotten barley
that stood in the school grounds,
separating out the still useable grains.
Every day I was imprisoned in a stench of decay
and there, under scorching sun and in beating rain,
I realized I was all alone in the world.
Soon after those three months of punishment were over,
during ethics class Headmaster Abe said:
"We're winning, we're winning, we're winning!
Once the great Japanese army has won the war,
    in the future
you peninsula people will go to Manchuria, go to China,
and take important positions in government offices!"
That's what he said.
Then a B-29 appeared,
and as the silver four-engined plane passed overhead
our Headmaster shouted in a big voice:
"That's the enemy! They're devils!" he cried fearlessly.

But his shoulders drooped.
His shout died away into a solitary mutter.
August 15 came. Liberation.
He left for Japan in tears.

Runny

Nobody's around, they're all out working.
A small kid left on his own squats
beneath the eaves, playing with a worm.
After that, once the worm's gone,
he digs up some earth to gnaw,
and plays, just plays.
The whole village is empty.
One plump hen
is there on its own too.
The kid's on his own too.
He's not been put on the family register yet,
not even been given a name but
he often has the runs so he's called Runny, Runny.
After playing there alone
he falls asleep on the bare ground
then the shade moves away, so he wakes up
and cries a bit.
Nobody knows he's crying
but —
that's not loneliness, it's trust.

A growing trust, though he's left on his own.
The trust that's in harmony with the world,
though he plays all alone.
How else would they dare?
Poor little Runny!
How else would they dare?
How else would they dare?

Lee Chong-nam

When children cry, if you tell them:
"A roaring tiger will come,
a big tiger will come
and carry you off if you cry!"
the crying goes on.
But if you say:
"They'll take you to Sinpung-ri police box!"
then the crying stops as if by magic.
And grown-ups too,
when they pass before Sinpung-ri police box
with the three trays of eggs they're selling,
they feel as if they've stolen them somewhere, and
their hearts beat two or three times faster than normal.
One fellow simply took to his heels
as he went by and was called in: "Hey, you!"
by a Japanese cop, and had a hard time.
I had a fright going by there once, too,
as I was following Uncle Hong-sik
on the way to sell dried pine branches
down at the wood store.
A man coming out had a messed-up face,
hands tied behind his back.

He was being transferred to Kunsan
    Central Police Station.
Someone was marching along behind him,
    holding the rope.
And who was that?
The police box cat's paw, that's who,
Lee Chong-nam,
brother-in-law to our grandfather's niece.
That wicked man!
He kicked his wife in the stomach and made her abort.
He turned on his own father and pulled his beard.
But where the Japs were concerned, he was down
    on his knees,
on his knees and crawling, he was so crazy about them!
At Liberation he should have been first to get it,
but he hid for a while, and when he came out
he was put in charge of Sinpung-ri police box.
He dressed himself up in a policeman's cap and uniform,
and put on airs riding around the district on a bicycle:
Tring-a-ling, tring-a-ling,—"Out of my way!"

Scarecrow

In the autumn field the scarecrow looks like a visitor.
In the winter field the scarecrow looks like a beggar.
But not at all.
When you count the villagers, one, two…
you have to count the scarecrow too.

Sang-sik's Blind Mother

Midsummer. No matter how wide you open the doors,
pierce as many holes as you like in your mud walls,
still there's not a cool spot anywhere.
Then all of a sudden
comes a rumble of thunder from distant
  Yŏngpyŏng Mountain
and a moment later
the swish of a cool breeze, a ghostly wind.
With that comes a cataclysmic downpour
like Koguryŏ's General Kaesomun and all his army
like Paekje's General Kaebaek and all his army
like General Yushin of Silla and all his army,
but what army do we have around here?
Nothing to cover on the storage terrace, even.
The empty jars up there,
old Grandma,
her little grandchildren, are all quite soaked in the rain—
her dry withered breasts drenched,
the little boys' balls too all quite drenched.

Sang-sik's blind mother
together with her grandchild:
"*Aigu!* It's so cool, so cool,
so cool!"

A Ghost

Until I was ten I hovered between life and death.
In those ten years I grew wizened and old.
Once I was asleep, around midnight, a ghost would appear.
I screamed
and lay bathed in cold sweat
while Father woke up naked,
fetched a sickle
and hung it on the wall in the early light.
"Just let that ghost try to come back again.
I'll beat it to death.
I'll beat it to death!"
I was haunted by the ghost till I was more than ten.
The nights when the ghost walked were long, so long.
The next day's daylight,
the daylit trees and plants and distant hills,
none of them could rid me of my fear.
What finally put an end to that ghost
was when I no longer had to go hungry,
when I started to eat three meals a day,
when I was no longer sick with worms
wriggling in my stomach.

What's a ghost?
I know.
It's starvation.
I know.

Okya, the Palace Woman

Chosŏn era palace women were obliged to sleep sitting in
    a curtsy.
They were obliged to sleep with hands raised
as if about to rise from a deep prostration
with both fists pressed to the forehead.
Because if ever the king should appear,
just once in a lifetime,
they were obliged to rise
as they were, with opened eyes,
from a curtsy, with both hands to the brow.
What kind of a rule is that?
What kind of a palace rule is that?
At the end of the Koryŏ Dynasty, palace women
were in the same situation.
If ever a king had no son,
well-featured men would be chosen
and all the court women would be made pregnant
then just one of the babies would be chosen;
all the remaining fathers, mothers, and babies put
    to death.

Lady Okya gave birth to a daughter in that way
but somehow managed to survive,
escaped from the court
and lived as a simple commoner
with her husband and child.
Yes, people experience
stormy fates.
One in ten thousand
One in a hundred million.

Firefly

Summertime firefly, you're a simpleton.
You go dashing through life like an arrow, then die.
And you're the female simpleton that takes him
and has his kids.
Young Sunt'ae
and Chaehwan's little girl over in Chungttŭm
used to catch fireflies
and put them inside a gourd flower as a lantern
then with that feeble light
they used to play husband and wife
and nighttime housekeeping.
Time passed
and Chaehwan's daughter married a Kunsan stationer
while Sunt'ae remained an old bachelor, and went
to prison for assaulting someone when he was drunk.
Childhood things all left behind,
one of them became just an ordinary housewife
and gave birth to a few babies,
the other was taken into custody, judged,
and put on prison garb.

But one day another old bachelor
got put in the same prison cell.
Lo and behold, he came from the house
next door to the Kunsan stationer's store.
Talking and talking,
at last the talk turned to the housewife there.
Her husband, he said,
had given her four kids and yet
he'd been with the bar-girl too
and made her a baby as well,
and every time he came home drunk
he would knock his wife all over the floor.
At which Sunt'ae's eyes filled with tears.
Goddammit! As soon as I get out of here
I'll tear off his prick, and his balls as well!
But after a year in prison the firmest resolves
all just vanish into thin air, you know.
Nightingales sing, then fly away.

Sinch'on Church

The seats in the church on the hill above Sinch'on
are in the shape of a V,
women on one side
and men on the other,
with the preacher standing at the point.
When the preacher declared: "Blessed are the poor
  in heart,"
a sound of weeping would rise from one side
while the other side stayed unmoved.
When the preacher prayed
one side would answer, "Amen"
while the other side stayed silent.
Finally the preacher left
and elder Cho Dal-yŏn from Sinch'on took the services.
A lot of people dozed, working folk
who would fall asleep if they ever sat down.
Elder Cho Dal-yŏn was better than the preacher.
He spoke sermons and prayers
without raising his voice
so as not to wake the nodding sleepers.
The chicken was better than the pheasant.

When his Bible was all worn out
elder Cho borrowed someone else's.
He was a good man.
The children liked him.
The neighborhood dogs liked him and wagged their tails.
On snowy
Sundays
when the bell rang *dong-dong*
the local kids and the dogs all came running
to the church on the hill
the church that gives out rice-cake
the V-shaped church
the dozing church.
"Wonderful, wonderful!"

Volume 4 (1988)

T'ae-hyŏn: A Faithful Son

They were the most dreadfully poor family in
 our neighborhood
and, in addition to poor, short-handed too, for Chung-gil,
the fourth generation of only sons, had only one son.
For the fifth generation, his son T'ae-hyŏn was an only
 son too.

T'ae-hyŏn's father kept coughing,
a hacking cough,
spitting up blood like a nightingale,
crawling out then crawling in and lying back down
with no money to pay for medicine.
At his wits' end,
fourteen-year-old T'ae-hyŏn
went along to the dispensary outside the West Gate
and got a free prescription for his father.
Then he set out on a round of all the herbal druggists
 in Kunsan:
the druggist out in Shinp'ung-ri,
the druggist in Ŏ'ŭn-ri beyond Kaesa-ri,
the druggist in Sŏnjei-ri,

twenty druggists, more than twenty,
and by appealing to their sympathy obtained
one kind of tonic herb from each,
one kind of wild root from each,
one kind of everything.
Then he prepared the various medicines
in a pipkin propped on stones in place of a trivet.
After three years of sickness, color came back into his
    father's face.
Thanks to his treatment the sound of coughing vanished,
banished from T'ae-hyŏn's house,
the only son for the fifth generation,
even on the chill spring nights while apricots bloom.
Ah, the apricots are blossoming.
Tomorrow morning they'll be dazzling,
dazzling.

Old Jaedong's Youngest Son*

You wonder how on earth such a tiny thing can sing
    so well.
Even his father's own version of *Yukjabaegi*
he sings more artfully than his father himself.
Soaring higher and higher, late summer
    dragon-flies swarm.

Samdŏk's Grandmother in Wŏndang-ri

If you pass behind the bier-shed, on past
    Wŏndang-ri village,
at the top of the young pine grove in Wŏndang-ri
stands Samdŏk's family house.
With autumn work barely completed,
it's the first to have a new thatch roof,
that yellow house, that shining house.
Samdŏk's mother's nickname is "Dusting."
If her son's father-in-law comes on a visit from his
    distant home,
as soon as he leaves she dusts the place where he sat
and dusts it again the next day,
muttering at the least excuse: "It's dirty here, it's
    dirty there."
Everywhere is spotless — corners of rooms,
the yard outside — without exception anywhere.
No point in local spiders ever thinking
of spinning their webs in that house.
No point in local dust ever thinking
of settling carelessly in that house.

In that unluckily spotless house
the spirit of smallpox skillfully gained entry
and that was that!
Samdŏk's mother lay lingering in her sickness,
confined for one month, two months, more.
Even while she was confined to her bed,
she kept a wet rag and dry duster near at hand
and after visits from the doctor
from outside the West Gate
she would wipe the spot where he'd been sitting.
Finally she gave up the ghost.
Her eldest son Sam-nyong drank his fill,
then when she was being laid out
he placed a few dusters in her coffin, blubbering:
"Mother! Dust away up there to your heart's content."

Kim Sang-sŏn from Araettŭm*

The two brothers Kim from Araettŭm, Sang-mun
   and Sang-sŏn,
were the pride of the neighborhood,
not only for stubbornness, but for miserliness as well.
No one ever once went to their house
and succeeded in borrowing a rake.
No one was ever offered so much
as a steamed cabbage root to eat in that house.
When sweet potatoes were being steamed at Sang-mun's,
all the doors were shut tight. The family ate alone.
Perhaps because the younger can never equal the elder,
Sang-sŏn, the younger, went one better
and on mornings after neighbors had celebrated offerings
for the dead,
he could be found running here and there uninvited,
dropping in for a bite to eat,
and only leaving after getting a good meal,
to say nothing of three full cups of early-morning wine
to wash down the steamed fish.
When his kid wanted to eat taffy
and filched scrap iron,

old bits of plow,
or bits of hand-scales to exchange for taffy,
then got caught, and sworn at: "You thief!"
he would side with him and say,
"The minute you eat taffy it turns into flesh and bones,
so come on, what's the use of yelling at the rain?"
As for Sang-sŏn's family affairs,
they never knew a lean year.
Things never went badly for that family
until the year after the start of the Pacific War
when Sang-sŏn's wife was crossing an icy patch
with a water-crock on her head. She slipped,
she and the crock went crashing down,
and off she went to the world beyond.
Not one of the local lads offered to help carry the bier.
Bearers were hired at great expense of blood and tears
but then it was as if the banners and streamers
    were starched,
giving not so much as a flutter
as the bier moved off.

Elder Cho's Wife

Cho Kil-yŏn from Saemal, over the fields from Kalmoe,
received a huge stretch of paddy and rich land at
   his marriage
but he squandered it all.
Now he earns his living farming someone else's paddy,
or rather he entrusts it to his lazy wife and pretends to
   farm it.
Yet this Cho Kil-yŏn sings nothing but hymns.
Even in the outhouse, it's hymns he hums
and Elder Cho's wife is just the same.
For laziness, she's first cousin to a maggot,
outdoing any outhouse-fed grub.
Even if cursed late-autumn rain comes pouring down
on the buckwheat on straw mats, the red beans on
   small mats,
she lies stretched out full length on the warmest part of
   the floor,
and if anyone opens the door, she cries:
"*Aigu*, what awful rain, what rain!
Well, cold rain makes a man, they say, and it makes
   grain tasty."

Then she gently summons sleep again.
As if she were descended from some leisurely angler,
she gently summons sleep again.
Meanwhile Elder Cho's daughter, Sun-bok,
works as hard as she can.
She comes flying across their rented field
like a butterfly,
like a bee on a radish flower,
scoops the grain out of the yard,
rolls up the sodden sacks, piles them in the store-room.
At which, good heavens!
faint late-autumn sunshine emerges,
banishing all thought of rain.

Beggars: Husband and Wife

In times when they have no food left
they go roaming around five villages:
Okjŏng-gol, Yongdun-ri, Chaetjŏngji,
Chigok-ri, and beyond Sŏmun —
no, six, including Tanbuk-ri in Oksan County:
"If you've any food, please, could you give us a spoonful?"
Their humility is so much humbler by far than
even the wife from Sŏnun-ri in Jungttŭm could manage.
The words "please, could you give" are scarcely audible.
During the bleakest days of harsh spring famine,
when they cannot see so much as the shadow
of a pot of cold left-over barley-rice, they say:
"Let's go drink some water instead."
Off they go to the well at Soijŏngji
to draw up a bucketful. Then those two beggars,
husband and wife, lovingly share a drink, and go
    home again.
In the twilight, thick flocks of jackdaws settle.
Daylight fades into twilight
as husband and wife pass over the hill at Okjŏng-gol.
In the twilight, smoke from a fire cooking supper
rises from only very few houses.

The Widows of Chaetjŏngji

If you ask for the widows' house in Chaetjŏngji,
it's well-known everywhere.
In that widows' house
live a widow of eighty
and her elderly daughter-in-law of sixty-four.
Both buried their husbands early on,
then planted plantains and balsams along the fence
and lived peacefully together like elder and
    younger sister.
At last the mother-in-law, being old,
grew chronically ill.
Her daughter-in-law cleared away her excrement.
She had difficulty in even clearing her throat of catarrh
and what a stench of old piss on the reed mat!
The daughter-in-law seemed to grow older,
her back bent
but even on snowy days she went wandering over
    sunny slopes
grubbing up shepherd's-purse roots,
always serving her mother-in-law.
When she boiled those roots in bean-paste soup,
the perfume spread throughout all the village.

Father's Second Sister Ki-ch'ang

She got married.
Abandoned, she returned home.
She crushed balsam flowers to dye her nails.
She dyed all ten finger-nails,
saying nothing,
shunning even heaven far above.

Maternal Grandfather

Ch'oi Hong-kwan, our maternal grandfather,
was so tall his high hat would reach the eaves,
scraping the sparrows' nests under the roof.
He was always laughing.
If our grandmother offered a beggar a bite to eat,
he was always the first to be glad.
If our grandmother ever spoke sharply to him,
he'd laugh, paying no attention to what she said.
Once, when I was small, he told me:
"Look, if you sweep the yard well,
the yard will laugh.
If the yard laughs,
the fence will laugh.
Even the morning-glories
blossoming on the fence will laugh."

Su-dong and the Swallows

Su-dong's only family is his parents.
When they're out at work
and he is playing, alone,
looking after the house, he gets bored.
Home alone, his only sport is idly pulling weeds,
until every year in early spring the swallows arrive.
Filling up the empty house, the swallows become
    his family.
As the swallows fill up the empty house,
droppings fall on Su-dong's head.
The brood hatches, then in the twinkling of an eye,
the chicks grow up
and go their separate ways,
at which he finds himself bored again.
The yard is suddenly that much bigger.
Late in autumn the swallows,
setting off to fly fast over hills and seas,
over seas and oceans,
the swallows leaving for lands beyond the river,
for distant south seas,
gather on the neighborhood's empty washing lines

and sit in rows, preening their breasts with their beaks
before setting off.
Looking up at them all, Su-dong feels utterly lonely.
Feeling lonely
means growing up.
"You're leaving now, you'll be back next year.
Good-bye for now."
He gives each of the swallows a name:
Chick-sun,

      Chick-ku,

           Cheep-sun,

                Cheep-bo.

Blind Pul-lye

Over in Chaetjŏngji, Mun Chong-an's daughter
lost her sight when she was two.
She's twenty-six now, and nobody wants to marry her.
She's all the time wiping the step
or guarding the house, while her elderly parents,
backs bent, are out in the fields.
She guards the house, but there's nothing to guard.
That's when troublesome kids catch a beetle,
and come in asking: "Would you like some cake?
Open wide!"
They pop the beetle in her mouth and run away.
That's when bothersome neighbors sneak in
and slyly feel blind Pul-lye,
remarking: "My, how pretty you are,"
daring to lay a hand on her breast,
exploring beneath the hem of her skirt,
while desperately she tries to avoid the worst.
Yet she never once cries out
but suffers this act and that
in silence.

Once those adults,
those animals, rather,
have come to their senses and gone back home
and only then, alone, she weeps.
Even blind eyes have tears.
She cries a single tear drop.
A spider drops down
and hangs immobile at the end of its thread.

Chŏng-du's Mother

As the wife of a former county chief,
she's used to being entertained all around
but she's easygoing and kind,
so on days when the fields are being plowed,
plowed by a hired plowman,
she won't ask other people to fix his lunch,
but instead comes out hersself,
carrying the basket perched on a pad of reeds
on her ever so prettily combed-back hair.
As the plowman eats
she keeps insisting: "Taste this fish!
Here, try these vegetables."
Good days full of sunshine,
the ridges stretching between the fields and
the fresh earth emerging where fields have been plowed
enjoy the fresh wind,
buried maggots come crawling out, while
the lovely flesh beneath the light linen jacket is still.
So still, so still, and breathing!

Great Wen, the Peddler

Springtime,
in springtime,
when the first sprouts appear in icy fields,
the first visitor is unfailingly Great Wen the peddler.
When he turns up with a wen
the size of a small zucchini
on his left cheek
all the neighborhood kids come swarming.
The moment Great Wen sets down his pack,
they all come swarming.
All his odds and ends are dazzling.
All the girls long to have a hair-pin
a little mirror
the farm-boys are eying a reel for the string of a kite.
A moment later
the peddler starts to browbeat them all:
"You good-for-nothings, now that's enough staring.
If you look too long, you'll wear them out."
Then he slams his pack of wares shut
after which a few kids rush away then come back.

Yet no matter how much Great Wen hawks his wares
he finds it hard to eke out a living
for no one can pay for his goods, even with rice or barley.
The peddler's rough beard bristles in complaint.
He even goes so far as to curse the place:
"The year before last or last year even
this cursed village had no mind to buy my goods—
a no good place, a filthy place."
But the local kids are a year older now,
and when spring comes again
invariably that very first visitor comes again.
On arrival he's determined.
He's brought a big bag of sweets for the kids:
"Here's for you,
                    here's for you,
                                        here's for you,
here's for you." as he distributes the sweets.
If a child has a cold and can't come out,
he gives the child's sweet to its brother or sister.
Then once he's on good terms with all the kids,
one odd one
touches his wen and dashes away.
"You bastard, I'll have your balls off!
Bastard!"

Ummh-Hmm

I wonder if they called him Kyŏng-sul
after the name of the year he was born?
Anyway, old Master Kyŏng-sul,
passing sixty,
seventy,
never contradicts anything people say:
"Ummh-hmm."
Even if his daughter-in-law says one thing
today and another tomorrow: *Ummh-hmm.*
And his daughter-in-law
finds fault with his constant *Ummh-hmm*
after wetting the re-papered windows with water
spat from her mouth
she scolds
father-in-law
and husband in a single breath,
yet he shows no emotion:
Ummh-hmm.
Entering the stable
to cover a cow's back with straw matting
he hits his head on the cow's horn:
Ummh-hmm.

He emerges, leaving a trail of dung.
Neighborhood kids
tease old Master Kyŏng-sul's grandson:
"Hey, come here, Ummh-Hmm."
"Have some dung instead of cake, Ummh-Hmm."

Kil-nam

Out he goes to play in early spring in the icy fields
only he can't go anywhere,
it's all still blocked by snowdrifts,
so he stays indoors blocked by the cold, the scorn of
    the family.
Then out he goes to play in the fields in early spring
when the melting snow is trickling away
until: *Aigu!*
In the sheltered corner of a tiny ditch
he glimpses a clump of floating frog-spawn.
Maybe he's afraid someone may challenge him for it?
He quickly scoops it up in the palm of his hand,
where it seems ready to slip back to the ground,
and slurps it down.
Kil-dong's younger brother Kil-nam,
ever inseparable from the grime on his heels,
obliged to live with nothing to wear, nothing to eat
but scraps,
grows up well
with never a cold,
only a flaw in his slanting eye,
only a fake stomach ache.

Ask him what he wants to do in life,
he replies, "Of course, surely, like father, like son"
in a grown-up voice
with protruding lips.

Hyŏn-jo and Hyŏn-gak

It is hard for brothers to live in harmony,
even if they cultivate the Way.
Look how, after scheming together
and taking power,
Ch'oi Ch'ung-hŏn
finally slaughtered his brother Ch'ung-su.
Long ago, on the frontiers of Silla, two brothers,
Hyŏn-jo and Hyŏn-gak, both monks, lived on good terms,
on good terms like two persimmon trees side by side.
They shaved their heads together,
went into the hills and sat in cloud-wrapped halls,
then crossed the sea together and went to T'ang China
where they studied together.
Then together they crossed over mountains and plains
until they reached the great monastery of Bodhgaya to
    the west,
where both brothers attained Buddhahood.
If one of them smiled,
the other couldn't help but smile too.

Hŭi-ja

With hands still wet from washing dishes, she goes out
to the black alder grove and cries to her heart's
    content until

her dead mother's face appears. Star-seed sprinkled in the
    sky, stars appear.

Ch'am-man

My second cousin Ch'am-man
is called Sŏk-t'ae in the family register
and Pyŏng-sŏk in the clan genealogy.
My second cousin Ch'am-man,
comes down the Chaetjŏngji road
holding a long stick, an A-frame on his back,
with an awesome load of wood, a load of dead branches
it took half the day to cut and stack.
Down he comes,
barely taller than a dwarf
the load of wood rocking and swaying to and fro
and you wonder where he gets his strength.
Ch'am-man's stack of wood is truly awesome.
Caught among the branches
is a white bell flower
and following that flower
comes one imprudent butterfly.
You're pretty too, and pretty awesome.

Kim T'ae-sik the Butcher

Go five *ri* and more,
go a full ten *ri*.
Once past Yongtun village you arrive in Shinp'ung-ri.
The primary school there is an old one,
with tall trees standing in a gloomy line.
In the yard where all the pupils used to assemble,
several would collapse with sunstroke.
Among them
was a kid called Kim Wu-gi,
the son of Kim T'ae-sik the butcher from Naun-ri.
His classmates
made fun of Wu-gi, calling him,
"Butcher Kid, Butcher's Kid,"
and sometimes "Dog-Butcher, Cow-Butcher."
Kim T'ae-sik the butcher
has forearms thick as a normal baby's body,
yet his son Wu-gi's forearms are so skinny,
perhaps taking after his mother or his mother's family,
that the doctor from Naun hospital feels sorry for him
whenever he has to give him a shot.

People from Yongtun and Mijei villages, Wŏndang-ri,
   and Dokjŏm
have no alternative: once or twice a year
they must go to the butcher's shop in Naun-ri.
They're so poor they rarely think of eating meat,
and even if they celebrate ancestor offerings often
they must discriminate —
but have to buy a bit of meat
for their father's offerings,
or their grandfather's, at least.
Now, if they use the habitual low form
in addressing Kim T'ae-sik the butcher.
"Give me a couple of slices of good meat, and quick,"
he gives them a bad cut.
But if a less haughty customer asks,
"Please would you give me a portion of meat,"
he slices off a piece of best steak
and throws in some soup bones for good measure.
And when they exclaim: "Why thank you,
that's very generous of you," he replies,
"Here you go. Boil it up and eat it!"
laying down his knife.
He's double chinned,
looks well-fed even when he's eaten nothing.

His belly's round,
looks well-fed even when he's eaten nothing.
His only worry is his son Wu-gi's feeble constitution
always the same
no matter how much knuckle-bone soup he feeds him.

Sŏng-mo's Luck in Love

Young Sŏng-mo from Wŏndang-ri is in love
with the daughter of Chin Du-sik from Mijei.
Chin Du-sik's remarkable daughter
with her hair in a long thick tress
goes hurrying over to Wŏndang-ri every evening
and clings to Sŏng-mo, unable to tear herself away.
She brings cake from the offering-table
but they completely forget to eat it,
as they cling together, embracing tightly,
unable to tear themselves apart.
The stars hang thick in the heavens
as they flatten the barley in the barley-field,
unable to tear themselves apart.
Finally Kim Chae-jun, the barley field's owner,
finding his barley crushed here and there,
went out to keep watch at night and there
were Hong Sŏng-mo from Wŏndang-ri
and the daughter of Chin Du-sik from Mijei,
unconscious of everything in the world:
"Wretches!
         You wretches!

You've not only crushed the barley of a bad harvest,
you're guilty of promiscuity! I'll kill you for this!"
and went after them with his stick.
At which Sŏng-mo thought quickly and shouted:
"Kill me if you must but
let us finish what we were doing first."
At which the lifted stick was lowered:
"*Yeuch*, what a pair!
This stick's too good to be wasted on the likes of you."
The owner of the barley field went home and began
   a rumor
which spread like wildfire.
In a flash it came to the ears of Chin Du-sik.
He cut a piece of firewood
and thrashed his daughter on her legs
then locked her up in the back room.
Two months later, seeing her with morning sickness,
he hastily married her off in a shotgun wedding
to her young man in Wŏndang-ri.
Arrangements were being made to marry her to
   someone else,
her father preparing to take as son-in-law
the son from the general store at P'almajae in Kunsan
but children never want what as their parents want.

So far so good. Yet less than a year
after Hong Sŏng-mo had married Chin Du-sik's daughter,
and before she had reached the end of her
   postpartum period,
he'd already taken up with another girl
and put a baby in her belly too.
You could smell a lot of seaweed soup for nursing mothers.
Hard times.

Chin-su*

Chin-su is four years old,
the son of Kim Sang-bok over at Saet'ŏ.
Chin-su's parents had him after taking tonics.
"How cute he is!"
"*Aigu*, what a marvel!"
"He's a miracle to be sure!"
"*Aigu*, he looks good enough to gobble up!"
"A dragon hatched in a carp's nest!
A dragon hatched in a serpent's nest!
Even if a beauty like Chun-hyang
gave birth to a son,
he'd be nothing compared to this one!"
The local women kept on like this
but one day Chin-su disappeared completely.
His parents raised their voices, called for him.
One month passed, then a second month,
they were haggard with grief
when one evening Chin-su
was heard calling "*Ŏmma, Ŏmma!*" outside the gate.
"Who's that?" they called and went running out:
"It's a dream! He's alive!" They hugged him tight.

No doubt about it, it was Chin-su,
all haggard and gaunt.
"Chin-su!"

They asked here and there
and found that an old couple without any sons
living outside the West Gate
had taken little Chin-su.
They treated him like their own son
but the child refused to eat.
He kept crying all the time.
When he saw the fire burning in the kitchen hearth
he called out, "Ŏmma, Ŏmma"
and kept crying all the time
until at last they had no choice
but to bring him back in a covered basket.

"Shall we report that old couple outside
the West Gate to the authorities?
Shall we tear out their hair?"
After pondering over what should be done,
in the end their anger evaporated:
"We've got Chin-su back, that's all that matters."

And
high in the trees the magpies
are busily tearing apart an old nest
to build a new one,
bustling about on a cold day.
"We've got Chin-su back, that's all that matters."

A Traveler from P'yŏngan Province*

That traveler left
after sleeping just one night
in Taegil the farmhand's room near our house,
rain pouring down.
That traveler left, saying, "I'll be back."
One year passed, then a second, and a third,
but the traveler never returned.
He held himself bolt upright
and thrust his body forward when he pissed.
He told the little children
very politely,
"You little masters should visit Myohyang Mountain
     one day."
That traveler,
his forehead dripping with water from the eaves.

Ch'ae-sun

Pok-sun's youngest sister, Ch'ae-sun,
picked a peony at Chae-nam's house
and brought it home.
"You little wretch,
what can we do with flowers in this house?
If you're going to steal,
make it a sack of rice, at least!"
Ch'ae-sun's mother (what a woman!)
threw the flower down the drain
and Ch'ae-sun, lying with her feet pointing toward
    the yard,
complained, crying: "You threw the peony away."
Ch'ae-sun, always so fond of flowers,
became a whore near the airfield during the war,
wearing lots of clothes embroidered with flowers.
Her father died collaborating with the enemy.
Her mother died too.
And when Ch'ae-sun cooked rice
it was always full of stones.

When peonies bloom and fade
a hot wind suddenly rises.

Volume 5 (1988)

Kushirŏng Pass*

Up past the silkworm village in Okjŏng-gol,
outside the West Gate, at Kushirŏng Pass
lies the almost invisible tomb of an old man
    from Kushirŏng,
a tomb so worn down as to be almost invisible.
Was it ten years ago?
Fifteen?
The harvest failed and that old man from Kushirŏng,
unable to survive, soon starved to death.
The old man drank some water,
took to his bed, and died.

That old man from Kushirŏng, insulted all the time
by all the locals,
constantly mocked
by all the locals,
kept his lips sealed
and suffered through it all.
Then once he was all alone,
having gathered a load of hay

and piled it on his A-frame, as he went
    plodding homeward,
once he was alone,
at such moments
he went mumbling and grumbling down the twilight road,
complaining to himself,
imitating a confrontation:

"What a malicious slur! Outrageous.
Outrageous. What enormous grudges you must bear.
Oh, outrageous.
Instead of finding fault with me
go home and punch your fist against the ceiling."

Busy grumbling to himself,
he'd pass his own house without realizing it
and it was only when his load of hay
struck the corner of the wall round another house
that he'd cry out: "Oh, I've gone too far!"
Then the old man from Kushirŏng would make his
    way back,
that old man, his lower lip dangling.

Why should such a fellow
have been so very dull?
He was a cousin of water,
or of watered-down soy-sauce,
and after he returned to the dust,
dead of starvation,
how should he not feel bitter resentment?
When the weather is bad,
when the raindrops drop gloomily,
still the old man from Kushirŏng invariably
mumbles and grumbles up at Kushirŏng Pass.

After hearing his voice as they cross the pass,
feeble people
are sick for a fortnight,
sometimes even for a month or more.

That very worn-down tomb!
On Harvest Moon Day, when everyone plays,
the children from Okjŏng-gol go up there
and frolic freely all over it,
that tomb of the old man from Kushirŏng
up at Kushirŏng Pass.

The Orphan of Paekun Mountain

Early in the winter of 1951
during a battle at Paekun Mountain,
the South Chŏlla Province band of partisans
lost the captain of the local citizens' council,
Kim Chŏng-su, during a punitive operation by forces
from the capital division.
Kim Chŏng-su's son was
in the womb of his wife Lee Kong-ju, in the hills,
the head of the school of the South Chŏlla band,
Lee Kong-ju, graduate from Kangdong Political Institute.
She was later captured alive
and before mounting the scaffold in Kwangju Jail
gave birth to a son in her cell.
Then she was executed.

The new-born baby had already lost his father,
now he lost his mother too.
Luckily, a warder who had no son
adopted the child as his own and took care of it.

Seeing a baby was in her womb,
they did not shoot her on the spot.

That's how Lee Kong-ju, the partisan, was captured alive.
Born in Kongju in South Ch'ungch'ŏng Province,
so from early on called "the Kongju Comrade,"
she graduated from Kongju Teachers' College,
went to Moscow to study, came back
known only as "the Kongju Comrade"
having killed her own name for the revolution's sake.
In the police records
the Kongju Comrade
turned back into Lee Kong-ju, age 28.
At the time of the first, successful communist invasion,
she was in charge of North Chŏlla Province,
then took to the hills and was deployed in the
    Chŏlla band.

The child of Kim Chŏng-su and Lee Kong-ju grew up
and lived a quite different life.

The Couple Running the General Store

If ever I pay a visit to the General Store
in the Old Market at Kunsan, accompanying my Dad,
I'm all excited and in high spirits for several days after.
The General Store stocks everything from everywhere
and the couple who run it are truly well-matched.
The wife looks a bit like an ox,
angry-looking with her always blue-rimmed eyes.
She caught a thief who came to the store,
knocking him down and out in a flash.
Sometimes her husband
is so kind as to give an extra measure
to someone asking for more,
at which his wife appears, exclaiming:
"Just look at him!
From what thighs comes all that generosity?"
Yet still she always covers the bowl of rice with a lid
before serving her reed-like husband's meal.
She says:
"If I simply put rice in a bowl and served it up to
　　my husband,
what dignity would there be in our home?"

Yet at times she appears in the store
shouting at the top of her voice
and astounding people who have just struck a bargain:
"Why, if you keep beating down the prices like that,
a log will soon be a pair of chopsticks!"
She's equally sharp with the owner
of the Five Dragons Store next door:
"You will send us some customers today, won't you?"
She's as familiar with him as her own husband.
They've been neighbors for dozens of years.
Naturally the fellow is half way to being her husband.

That Fellow, Hong-nae

That fellow, Hong-nae,
hangs around Kunsan Station,
snatching a bite to eat here and there,
grabbing what he can,
sleeping better
curled up on a bench in the waiting-room
than in any soft quilted bed.
If he's caught going through some traveler's bundle,
he rubs his hands together begging for mercy
so hard that sparks start to fly,
weeps tears like chicken shit from both eyes
begging for mercy,
and when he's finally released
his face is full of beaming smiles,
as if asking: When did I ever beg or weep?
I wonder if he's ever washed?
Did he ever take a bath?
If just left to himself
he's sufficiently dirty
and sufficiently clean.

That fellow, Hong-nae,
who learned as a kid all about wretched life,
is accustomed
to pray
fit to bust
and when he laughs
he laughs standing straight as a tombstone.
And on days when it freezes hard
no ear muffs protect his red ears,
that fellow Hong-nae
down at Kunsan Station.

Chae-sŏn's Mother

On cold days
icily cold days with hail spitting down,
loveliest in our neighborhood, Chae-sŏn's mother
loveliest and youngest in our neighborhood,
    Chae-sŏn's mother
her tiny face
full of smiles
full of sorrows,
perhaps coming back from her parents' home
which has not so much as a fence,
carrying little Chae-sŏn on her back
with the carrying-blanket wrapped high around her
and Chae-sŏn waking from sleep in the dark inside
borne along with the darkness,
when she encounters neighborhood men on the path
she steps aside, bows low,
and if they greet her:
"Are you on your way back from somewhere?"
replies in a tiny voice
"Yes, from my parents' house,"
so quietly they cannot hear.

If someone asks for a loan, she replies:
"Here, use this before I do," and hands it over,
even if it's money she's just borrowed for herself,
"Why, there are others poorer than me."
Sometimes the local menfolk examine
Chae-sŏn's mother's face closely:
"How can you stay so pretty eating nothing but barley?"
And though they tease her
she never scowls, replies instead:
"Keep your praises for my little Chae-sŏn."
Her eyes are calm, full of dreams, perhaps,
or the rising tide,
and with that limpid gaze
she diligently serves her bitter poverty,
serves her half-paralyzed husband
through winter and all.
Doing laundry in deep midwinter
she plunges her frozen hands into the icy water,
the paddle beating the washing resounds,
echoing in fold after fold.

Pun-im from Mijei

In early morning Pun-im carries two buckets of water
on a yoke, her face bowed toward the ground,
Pun-im with her eyelashes so long.

Pun-im. There's no way of knowing what she's achieving
ten fathoms down deep in her heart,
as the hem of her black skirt soaks up the dew
and below it her busy feet soak it up too.

Pun-im, who never loses a drop from her water buckets.

Yi Yong-ak*

He left us the most painful and lovely of all
modern poetry written in our land,
he left us the most painful and truthful of all.
In the 1930s when we were under Japanese rule
he would stand, hungry,
in the center of Seoul,
waiting for anyone he knew to come by.
Soon after Liberation in 1945,
Sŏ Chŏng-ju published a volume of poems, *Nightingale*,
in praise of long journeys to Western realms
and went out to the publication party
dressed in a fine silk shirt.
Yi Yong-ak turned up at the party
and drew him into a corner:
"Chŏng-ju, a word in your ear."
Thereupon he pulled a knife from his belt
and slashed that fine silk shirt,
spat: "You hopeless bourgeois,"
and walked out.
If he was sent a pack of salted fish roes from home
in far north Hamkyŏng Province

he'd ask someone to look after them
and savor them little by little as he wandered about.
In the chaos of the late 1940s,
the days of chaotic poetry,
days when only flowers of sorrow bloomed,
he turned his back on every kind of scoundrel,
every kind of falsehood and trickery,
every kind of vice.
Those were days he could not endure.
With the 38th Parallel
cutting across our land's rivers and hills,
how could he think of his own safety?
Such was his destiny.
He left a few lines of poetry
then went to China, and farther, to the wild far north,
    to Russia,
or so his elderly neighbors reckoned —
to terrible places, anyway.
A man of poetry who never lied,
he shines out, a distant lamp shining
down a long night road.

Sang-sul's Mother-in-Law

Sang-sul's mother-in-law
arrives at her daughter's house
and makes life there harder still.
She eats one peppery beet for dinner,
a beet so peppery
she wants to say it's peppery but
even that's too much to say.
Instead she mutters: "If we don't burp after eating beets,
it's as if we've eaten wild ginseng."

No thought of leaving the next day, either.
She ought to be moving on to her son's house
but her daughter-in-law's always so petulant.
No thought of going back home.

All the while she's at her daughter's house
she's on friendly terms with everyone she meets,
seeming already familiar,
glad to see them.
Even if you turn into a four-footed beast
with your back bent double,
a lifetime lasts a long time.

Even if there's nothing to eat or wear,
even if you live in a room as full of drafts as a sieve,
life is long.
She's apparently proud
of being an eighty-year-old wreck.

That face's smile:
is that a smile? Or a pretence of a smile?
The pretence of a smile obliged to come out
at the mere sight of a shabby tree?

The Stones of Ŏch'ŏng-do

Far out in the West Sea
lies the island of Ŏch'ŏng-do,
lonely Ŏch'ŏng-do
surrounded by the sound of waves.
On Ŏch'ŏng-do
are twenty graves.
Before each grave stands a single stone.
The wives
carved their husbands' faces on the stones they raised.
Yet they don't look like portraits,
only stones, but still
maybe there's some kind of likeness.

They're the graves of men who died when a boat capsized
in the great tidal wave seven years ago.
In the midst of those graves
stand four empty ones
for the bodies of those never found.

Their sons
soon learned to roll up nets.

Following their fathers
they learned to catch fish.
As soon as they're fifteen
they'll be sailing off to catch croakers,
they'll be sailing off to catch hair-tail fish.

The Old Woman of Chaetjŏngji

That old woman's past sixty, past seventy,
yet her footsteps are light,
that old woman selling acorn-muk in Chaetjŏngji.
Her mind
has quite gone,
so when she sleeps
she dreams of her childhood
and her sleeping face is bright with smiles,
then after sweetly smiling she smacks her lips.
Sixty-five years all swept away,
that old woman dreams only of childhood,
when she wore ribbons in her hair.
If she wakes up,
"Heh-heh, ho-ho, heh-heh, ho-ho,"
the sound of her childhood laughter continues on.

Her face is a whole network
criss-crossed and covered with wrinkles.
Her laughter does not suit her face,
that "heh-heh, ho-ho" fit to shake the seeds
from the cockscomb flowers,

laughter like that of a silly, flighty young girl,
while the passing cow looks blank,
the donkey looks blank,
there's really no telling,
and the house's cockerel too shuts its eyes:
"Heh-heh, ho-ho."

Chin-ja's Older Brother

Chin-ja's older brother is a mass of pimples.
He loathes and detests schoolwork,
so when he's given a lunchbox
he goes off and idles the hours away under a bridge,
gobbles up the food in his lunchbox,
sleeps his fill,
brushes the dried grass from his clothes, then,
when it's time for the kids in school to come home,
he slowly sets his legs in motion.
He's truly a prodigal.
When he arrives back home,
their hard-working mother beams brightly
as she busily wipes the pots on the storage terrace:
"Are you back, then?
What did you learn today?
How much Japanese did you learn?"
"I learned five or six words."
"Come on, repeat them to me."
After a while, quite at a loss:
"Rice: *bento*
Teacher: *sensei*

Student: *gakkusei*

Rabbit: *usagi*

Morning-glory: *asakaho.*"

"There, my little treasure. What a blessing,
you've inherited all your father's gifts.
You're a gift from heaven come down to earth.
Aigu, what a fine thing for our family.
You'll turn into a great scholar, another Chŏng P'o-uˇn."
If someone who sees him playing under the bridge
    scolds him:
"Hey, you brat. What are you up to, not going to school?"
he replies, "I like farming more than school.
Cutting fodder and carting muck is what I like."
"You brat! In that case,
off you go to the meadows, off to the fields."

Chungttŭm Chae-su's Baby

For six years after the marriage, not a sign,
so she got harsh treatment from mother-in-law.
At last, well done, a baby started up,
so she got kind treatment from mother-in-law.
Then the baby was born with hardly a whimper.
The cord was duly buried on the hill behind the house.
That darling darling Chae-su's baby.

Except the new-born baby
seemed to have come into the world sick.
It could not catch its breath,
its throat was blocked,
it couldn't even swallow milk.

Here and there she ran,
to the Guam clinic run by an Englishman in Kunsan,
the Kaejŏng clinic in Kaejŏng county,
as well as to Chin's clinic:

"Please save our baby's life, at least."
Crazy girl,
crazy girl.

She went back to the Guam clinic
and they told her to take it home.
As she made her way home weeping and wailing,
clasping the dying child tight,
it grew stiff without one bone having time to harden.
"I'll follow it to heaven," she wept,
sank to the ground with the tiny corpse
and wept her heart out
until she was completely out of tears.
In a faint voice her husband Chae-su said:
"That's right,
go with it if you can.
That's my thought too."

To those still alive
a dead baby is so unforgettable.
Its enormous eyes!
Its wide, wide forehead!
Its very first laugh we longed to savor!
Aigu!

Chin-dong

Chin-dong from Mijei
used to be called Kim but
then his family name got changed to Chang.
Chin-dong followed his mother when she remarried
and grew big bones eating whatever he was given
in his stepfather's house.
If you're going to grow up like that
you need brains and other things too.
He was always forgetting everything
as if gongs were ringing in his head.
If he was assigned some task
even after being reminded two or three times,
he'd go out on some other task that day,
on an important errand for his stepfather,
sent on an errand to Sanbuk-ri, say,
but as he dashed past the ditch
beyond the shack where the Wŏndang-ri bier was kept,
he'd completely forget,
would come back home,
get a bowlful of oaths, then set out again.
This time he'd be crossing the log bridge

at the far limits of Wŏndang-ri before he forgot,
and come back home;
then his mother would put everything in order again,
murmuring that utter darkness is better than feeble light.
Then as he went along he would have it all together
in his mind and in his heart
but just as he was arriving at Sanbuk-ri
the sight of a shackled ox mounting a cow
made him utterly forget again.
Coming back home
this time he not only forgot the errand he'd been sent on,
he'd even forgotten he'd been sent on an errand.
He was playing in the water
with the other kids
when his stepfather glimpsed him
and all hell broke loose.

The neighbors said
his mum and dad were wrong
to send such a kid
all the way to Sanbuk-ri to buy a draft of liquor.
"Why, that kid
would miss enough even right before his eyes.
How come they send him so far? Really!"

Mun Ch'i-dal

When it comes to Mun Ch'i-dal from Kaesa-ri,
he's irreproachable, no fault to be found.
Only he's a bit too blunt,
so if you're from elsewhere, he looks very angry.
Yet his moods are quiet as midnight
and if you get to know him, you'll like him.

He invariably keeps a few few coins stuffed
in the side-pocket of his tobacco pouch.
Even when he goes to the outhouse
he feels obliged to take a few coins with him —
one never knows when the need might arise.

He serves his old mother quite simply.
His sons all eat their fill.
Perhaps the only bad thing's his wife's sharp tongue.
When harvest is done
he quickly renews the thatch on the roof, so all is snug
and the hens in his yard are generous too,
regularly laying eggs.

From one end of the year to another
You'll never once see him drink to excess.
That's how Ch'i-dal is.
So people tell one another: "If you're going to lend money,
lend to Ch'i-dal, the others will never pay you back."

That's how Ch'i-dal is. But one night
he was caught by bad spirits in the Kwanyŏn
    Hill cemetery.
Left leg and right
were given a hard time
and he lay paralyzed for several months,
during which time he never once saw the cow's
    bright face,
just lay in his room eating thin gruel
before he started to eat solid food again.

"Why, Ch'i-dal, you're out again!
After hiding all that while from the sun,
your face is pale as the inside of a gourd
and you've got yourself a new personality too."

Tta-ok

The house in the bamboo grove in Okjŏng-gol,
snug with the sound of wind among the leaves:
that's where pretty Tta-ok lives.
When the frozen rice-field had thawed
the shadow of the facing hill fell across it,
the shadow of the cherry trees blooming on the hill fell
     across it.
Pretty Tta-ok was watching,
Tta-ok with her black hair,
hair her mother would plait conscientiously
     each morning.
No one could mock her black blouse and
     watermelon-colored skirt.
Tta-ok always looked as if she were fresh from a bath.
The world was never rude to her.
If she went out alone to gather mugwort,
the mugwort would always be specially fragrant.
Pretty Tta-ok:
what thoughts
make Tta-ok smile all the time to herself?

Ssal-bong

Ssal-bong, daughter of old T'ae-ok:
Ssal-bong used to be always making dolls,
carrying them about like babies on her back.
When she grew bigger
Ssal-bong used to carry the neighbors' baby on her back.
Though her mother staged a hunger strike in opposition,
Ssal-bong rushed to join the man she'd chosen.
They took a room not far from Chaebo Wharf at Kunsan,
set up house there
but her new husband was broke and useless
so she rolled up her sleeves and set about
trying her utmost to make a living,
doing the cleaning in this house and that
and the washing too.
In the course of all that, a certain time passed
and her indignant mother gradually
turned down the heat, saving oil and softening up.
Finally, uncertain whether they were living on rice or
    just gruel,
she walked two miles
with a sack of rice on her head for them.

After asking and asking at Chaebo Wharf,
she found them living in a rented room
at the topmost house in P'almajae, and gave them
    the rice.
"Mother, you shouldn't bring such things.
Food tastes better if I work hard to earn it, Mother.
Mother, he's really virtuous." Apart from his virtue,
her husband has nothing to brag about.

Great-Aunt in Tangbuk-ri

As we left, kicking the dew, after spending a night there,
our warm-hearted great aunt would stand watching
as we faded into the far distance
until we were out of sight
over those wide fields.
She never once put on colored clothes,
always wore a plain white cotton dress,
her hair neatly combed back, slick with castor-bean oil,
held in place with a pin of jade.
Great-Aunt was always graceful.
If someone told her anything a little bit sad,
tears would flow
from both eyes
silently
tears would flow.

Two Blind People

In Chammi-dong, Kunsan, several blind people
    live together,
several blind people good at massage
living happily together.
If a call comes for one to go to some inn,
an old man takes a young blind girl along.
And although they hold walking sticks,
it's a familiar route, even if they can't see,
they take it all the time,
their sticks barely touching the ground.

That blind man's not her father, she's not his daughter,
but among them adoptive relations are firm.
The one wearing dark glasses and
not afraid if it rains, is the daughter.
The one with eyes wide open, not seeing a thing,
leading the way, is the father.

When no one's about
they talk in low voices
and laugh: something they otherwise never do.

Amidst all the world's evil
there is this goodness too:
even darkness can be a blessing!

Kim Ki-man from Mijei*

Kim Ki-man was the eldest son of rich Kim Chae-gu from
  Mijei.
From his father he inherited twenty thousand *p'yŏng* of
  paddy
as well as five thousand *p'yŏng* of fields,
all of which he frittered away
and came back home to live, destitute.

His ever so gentle mother
thrifty and diligent
did all she could to bring him up well
but it's hard for the son of a rich family to grow
  up properly.

From an early age, out he'd go, wearing tailor-made
  Western clothes
and make the rounds of the Kunsan bars,
coming home after taking his fill of fun.
tired and confused, he'd come back
after three days, or even six,
only after all his money was gone.

There's one person quietly watching Ki-man.
That's old Chae-gu's bastard son Ki-sŏn.
He may be only the child of a concubine,
but the neighbors are one in singing his praises.

No matter how madly Ki-man may be involved in his fun,
if he catches sight of his half-brother Ki-sŏn just once
he sobers up in a jiffy.
He turns away, muttering inside himself:
"You bastard kid, are you laughing at me?"

But Ki-sŏn's face is calm as a stream,
a stream without a breath of wind.

An Errand

One cold day
Nam-ch'ŏl is on his way home from some far-off errand.
No hood to cover his head,
his bare face is frozen.
Extreme freezing cold
makes his body grow warm
and suddenly the outside world is as snug as any room.
"You must be cold?"
"Not as cold as when I sit quietly inside my room
    at home.
It's better outside than in my room."

When he's in his cold, oppressive,
gloomy room, the paper covering its door
patched and grimy,
it feels so good
to be sent out on some errand.
On first setting out
his steps may not be so brisk
but once past Saet'ŏ,
once past Paupaegi

once he's out among the Paupaegi rice-fields
where you can see across to Kalmei,
on that freezing path amidst ice and snow
whipped by the wind till he seems about to fly off,
a warm power begins to flow inside him
and the cold cannot get to him.

All summer long
Nam-ch'ŏl from Soichŏngji
with his constant fevers
had no chance to be well.
But in winter Nam-ch'ŏl suddenly grows taller
and as he goes on errands all alone,
his heart beats faster than ever.

There's a girl called Sŏnja in the house he's off to.
Sŏnja has long eye-lashes
but the dog guarding that house is fierce.

The Women Preachers from Kunsan

The church in Kunsan's Kumsŏ-dong neighborhood
stands at the top of thirty steps.
That church has two women preachers.
One occasionally visits our village
hugging a Bible to her breast.
When the local women ask:
"Even if we want to believe in Jesus,
how could we ever go all the way to Kunsan?"
she simply smiles.
When the menfolk come along
and ask, "Is there a God?"
she replies: "If you call on God often enough,
He comes, even if He doesn't exist," and smiles.
Her hair is neatly slicked with camellia oil.
Her husband died
just after they married
so she took this path
and spends her life saying: "Believe in Jesus, believe."

But the other woman preacher from Kumsŏ-dong church
tells people:
"If you don't believe in Jesus you'll be damned.

Brimstone is a fearful thing,
you must believe.
If you want to cross the River Jordan
and enter Paradise,
believe in Jesus."
Now this woman preacher is the prettier of the two,
prettier than the one who visits our village.

One day three of the local children
stopped this preacher on her way:
"Don't visit our village.
If you come, bring us some sweets to eat."
The woman preacher smiled, and meekly went
    back home.

The Osŏng Mountain Stream

There's always water flowing in the stream at
  Osŏng Mountain,
shallow, but enough to keep a carp from dying at least,
and for the sake of that one stream
the hills to either side stretch far and wide,
the fields of Osŏng Plain here,
the side of Osŏng Mountain there,
gentle slopes there too,
and in the midst of them all
the stream flows on amid remote mountains.

For the sake of that flowing stream
the mountains divide,
proud though they are,
and as twilight falls reverently
crimson dusk tints the clouds
before they too
fade reverently into night.

At that moment the youths gathered in Osŏng Mountain
all those sweat-bathed youths

adjust their eyes to the starlight
and "Now, let's go!"
They carry bamboo spears.
And who's that youth out in front?

Beaten up yesterday by the Japanese farm owner
and bitten by the farm's dog,
it's the son of Ch'a Dong-ku from Shinjŏng village
in Nap'o County,
isn't it?

Tonight the trickling stream barely
makes a sound and toward that sound
one lone lamp shines at the Japanese farm, Mr.
Kunggi's farm.

Surely old Ch'a's son,
with that snub nose of his,
who refuses to get married
until he can buy a thousand *p'yŏng* of paddy,
surely the muscles in his arms are tense.
No question of paddies or fields tonight:
you die. I die.

Slowly the lamp comes closer.
A large dog begins to bark.
It bites at the darkness.
The stars look ready to fall from the sky.
Ready to fall and crash.
You die. I die.

Shin Man-sun

There's a small store at Hŭngnam-dong Hill
on the road from Kunsan to Kunggi's farm.
The son of the storekeeper, Shin Man-sun, still a child,
has a splendid chin to his rounded face.
His hands are splendid too.
Unknown to his mother
he passes out cookies to the local kids
as well as giving coins to the poorest ones.
Unknown to him,
his mother watches him
through the glass in the sliding door.
A moment later, after coughing in warning,
she emerges, apparently oblivious of everything.

"Man-sun, it's time to do your homework.
I'm going to take care of the store now."

Man-sun's father is gentle and kind,
Man-sun's mother even gentler and kinder.
What makes all the three of them the same?

Why, for some inexplicable reason
even the smoke from their chimney
is just like them,
the smoke from the chimney behind Man-sun's house,
rising so gently and kindly.

Chin-gyu's Grandfather

The magpies are building a new nest.
without ever pausing to rest,
busy magpies in the poplar tree.
Not just the immediate family,
but also the newly-weds
and even the neighbors are hard at work.
They're shifting their nest from this tree to that.
It takes more than three days to move.

Chin-gyu's grandfather, Sang-tu's dad,
on his way back from a stroll in the hills
pesters Sang-tu, the district clerk:
"Look at that, Mr. Clerk,
the magpies are moving their nest.
Why don't we go somewhere else too?"
Sang-tu's dad is in his dotage,
Chin-gyu's grandfather is seventy-three
and shakes his head spasmodically.

After his grandson Chin-gyu had taken a wife
he pulled open their door in the middle of the night:

"You young wretches!
How come you forgot to lock your door?
Were you in too much of a hurry?
Disgusting! Outrageous!"

Cousin Kŭm-dong

When he wasn't drunk
he was as bland as the white stuff
lining the inside of a bamboo.
He was as insipid
as the dust on an old cobweb.
His nose was never dry,
a trickle of snot was always hanging down.
He was so insipid
if a fly settled on him, he'd never wave it away.
Yet on top of all that,
if he went out on a drinking binge
you never saw the likes of him,
wilder than that stubborn bull over at Sang-sul's in Saet'ŏ.
He'd go around swearing at everyone,
though he made a distinction between skirts and pants.
On meeting the local women or his aunt:
"Ya, bloody bitches!"
and to the local menfolk:
"Bastards!
You big-balled bastards!"
Then after drinking more, he headed for Kunsan

and after drinking there he headed for Iri
and once in Iri
he took someone's bike and rode off on it
until he fell off
and was caught
and hauled off to jail
and only emerged after eight months inside.
Emerging from prison
he went roaming the coast along Mijei Dyke,
made up his mind
and started to farm.
He no longer touched a drop
but his nose, running since childhood, continued to
    do so
as he got himself a field to plant paddy,
planted out the rice,
and immediately began weeding it.
He no longer drinks
he's utterly dull.
On nights when the full moon shines down brightly
though dogs may bark
though someone makes a remark
he never replies, just looks up at the moon.
Falling asleep, he never dreams.

O-nam and His Wife

O-nam takes care of other peoples' affairs for free,
helps clear things up without stealing the limelight,
less than five feet tall, dwarfish O-nam.
His wife outshines him
taking care of the hard work in other peoples' houses.
If she hears of a death, she hurries off,
boils noodles for the visiting mourners,
sets up a barrel of wine in the yard: O-nam's wife.

When times are hard
all the other households are unfailingly stingy
but when people visit O-nam's place
he brings out many things without being asked.
If they go to borrow just a sack,
they get offered hard rice-cake as well, at least.
When it's time for winnowing, the basket seems to toss all
   by itself
for O-nam's wife is so tiny
she can't be seen behind it.
Still she separates out the grains with the utmost skill.

The local folk kid the two of them:
"O-nam, you don't have no wife at home —
you live with a mouse!"
"O-nam's wife, you don't have no husband at home —
you live with a dwarf!"
Everyone talks like that about the two of them.
But when O-nam's feeling happy
he's ready to help his wife beat washing for half a night.

Im Yŏng-ja*

The loveliest and brightest girl
in Wŏndang near Mijei,
already ripe at the age of ten:
Yŏng-ja.
As you pass the ridge between Wŏndang and Naun-ri
    in Tokchŏm
even the birds in the young pines are silent
and passers-by pause in spite of themselves.
Standing there,
Yŏng-ja would listen to anything they said as they passed.
Then the Reds came down.
She was forced to serve as a civilian officer
wearing a torn skirt.
And for the crime of having served the Reds
was abused by
this man
and that man,
and the police.
She was obliged to bite off her tongue and end her life.

No one knows where her grave is.
Once summer is gone, when sweet campanula bloom,
autumn sees chrysanthemums in flower.
Yŏng-ja was lovely as that when she used to smile.

Volume 6 (1988)

Ssangga-mae*

Ssangga-mae is the daughter of the barber at Sanbuk-ri.
Ssangga means "double-crown," which she's got,
and that's her name as well.
Ssangga-mae's quick at hide-and-seek,
good at skipping too,
and very good at "tugging at the reins"
with her pretty tongue just peeping out.
Very bold for a little girl,
she catches snakes,
frogs,
and she's not afraid of dogs.
Ssangga-mae soon learned to read and write.
She could read the classic story of Yu Ch'ung-yŏl.
Her completely illiterate granddad,
hearing her read that tale, murmurs proudly:
"My grandchild, my grandchild."
Perhaps because her father's a barber,
Ssangga-mae has always worn her hair in a bob.
Yet if she needs to piss
as she's walking down the highway,

she lifts her skirt, crouches down, and the waters flow
no matter who may be watching.
The heavens seem to sympathize
as they sparkle with summer lightning.

The Senile Old Man of Wŏndang-ri

Old Hong Dal-p'yo from Wŏndang-ri, being senile,
gets up
with a great deal of snorting
at the peep of dawn,
throws open the doors of this room and that,
rattles the handle of doors that are locked:
"What, aren't you ready to get up yet?
To sleep too long
is a sin second only to murder.
Come on!
If you behave like this,
how dare you eat
three meals a day?"
Once having started
he can't leave off for quite some time.
How on earth is that skinny wretch
so stuffed full of empty chatter?

As a matter of fact, even before he was senile
whenever he was alone his lips never stopped chattering
though he was a little quieter while he was eating,

but then, sure enough:
"Why must I speak out
even while I'm eating?
Well, that bitch mixed stones with my rice,
dropped hairs in the side-dishes.
What a daughter-in-law!
I suppose I'm lucky she doesn't try to kill me with lye.
What kind of son is that,
willing to live with such a woman?"

And if that wasn't enough, he'd turn to other woes:
"*Aigu,* if my dead wife heard of all this
on the days of her memorial offerings,
when her spirit comes for its portion of rice,
she'd go back drowned in her own tears
for pity at her husband's plight."

If meat soup was served,
old Dal-p'yo would scoop the meat
out of his son's bowl:
"How come nobody says a word?
Your husband gets all the best bits,
you no-good bitch."

"I'll probably die today
so don't go off to the fields. Stay home,
you wretches.
Today will see the end of me."

But nothing happened,
all day long.

Ch'ang-sun from Mijei

Her face white
as a frozen chestnut
overflowing with white happiness,
as she fills the long clothes-line
full of washing
her happiness overflows as she raises the clothes-pole
and turns into a song of happiness
in resonant tones:
"Sea birds fly over distant lands in the south…"

Hong Chong-wu*

He was the first Korean to study
at the Sorbonne in Paris.
He did well, then he abandoned
all he had learned
and turned into an assassin.
On his way back home
he trailed the Enlightenment Party's Kim Ok-kyun
from Japan to Shanghai, shot him dead
and sent his body back to Seoul,
where his head was displayed on a pole as a warning
    to traitors.

Hong Chong-wu the assassin returned home quietly,
and on the merit of his deed got a job as a
    low-grade functionary.
Then he established the Imperial Association in
    opposition to
the Independence Association and the Korean
    National Association,
sent peddlers to fight demonstrators and did
    outstanding service
sabotaging the Independence Association's operations.

The final years of the Chosŏn era
were embellished by such reactionaries,
and today too, all over the country,
their descendants flourish.

There's a place in history
even for people who betray history.

The Thief from Sonjei-ri

When he was on his way to commit a robbery
he'd first pay a visit to his grandfather's grave
and ask for help: "Grandfather, I'm off now.
Please watch over me, Grandfather."

Was that why? Maybe. Anyway,
he pulled off ten thefts and more before being caught.

His schoolboy son
was caught stealing at school,
three times, maybe four,
and inevitably got expelled, in the end.

Before his father had scored twenty, he too was in irons.

That thief's wife,
who was also a thief's mother,
went to visit him in prison, wept, came home
and pounded her son's
wrists with a club so
he could never use his fingers.

A Baby's Grave in Kalmoe

Less than a year old,
it had no name.

Emerging into the world,
it breathed a few times, then went away
before being entered on the family register.

Its mother, having no tears,
made no lament.

It was a hungry time, you see.
A dog came sniffing round its grave.
Finally it dug down into the earth,
ate the thing buried there, and went mad.

Two people got bitten by that mad dog.

That kid
without so much as a name
came into the world

and succeeded
in producing a mad dog.

Someone from Mijei killed the mad dog.

Wu-sik from Arettŭm*

His father left for Manchuria when he was small
so he couldn't remember what he'd looked like
and when he was twelve his mother quit life as well,
so little Wu-sik found himself
obliged to run the household.
Below him were his two younger brothers
Wu-jong and Wu-man.
He prepared the food
for all three little brothers to eat.
The neighborhood women
shared their food with them, at least to start with,
although really
there's no telling how long such generosity might last.

On cold days on mornings when the wind whistled
through the holes in the paper lining the door,
he'd get up undaunted by the cold,
brush the snow from the yard,
draw water from the ice-covered crock
and wash until steam
rose from his newly-washed face,
then he'd call: "Wu-jong, get up!

Wu-man, get up!"
People hearing that call would comment:
"Ah, those three kids are getting on well."

Going to their mother's grave in early April
on the day for spring offerings,
Wu-sik would weep in sorrow,
while Wu-jong stood looking on blankly
and Wu-man, who grew up
never able to lament properly, "Mother! Mother!"
sat pulling at the dry grass
and just gazed into the distance.

When Wu-sik went back down the hill after crying
    his fill,
he felt full of new energy.
The world might be too much for him,
still he had the energy to burrow down
and make a shelter for them all.

"Wu-jong!
Let's wager who'll reach the bottom first!
Yoi, ttong!"

'Yoi, ttong?' Isn't that Japanese?

The Outhouse Ghost

Even on fine days,
Yong-gil's mother's pretty face was always twisted into
    a scowl.
She always looked as if something was wrong.
If you greeted her politely in the morning:
"Have you had your breakfast yet?"
she would fire back:
"Why? Are you going to feed me if I haven't eaten?"
Yet inside she was different,
soft like the inside of a clam.
If a nearby family were starving,
she'd send over some rough dough cake, at least.

Yong-gil's mother
went to the outhouse one night
and got a scare from the ghost living there.
A few days later she took to her bed, sick.
She was sick from the fright the spirit gave her.
Hearing that she'd get better
if she bound scraps of straw from the outhouse to
    her forehead,
she duly tied some round her head and lay there, sick.

But a fatal disease is a fatal disease.
Her life was done, she died.
Absurdly, she died.
No need to be sad.
She died.

Yong-gil's father drank himself into a fury,
set fire to the outhouse,
rooted up the bowl beneath it
and filled it with clay, dug from the hill behind.

When that was done,
he sat astride the coffin enclosing his wife's body
and stayed there all night long.
Finally, being alive and human, sleep overtook him
so he fell forward and slept on the coffin.

The next morning,
when the bier was setting out,
he stood dumb in a corner of the yard:

"That damn woman! Heartless, leaving me here
    all alone."

A Mother

During the Japanese invasions of the 1590s,
caught among the fleeing population driven on and on,
then isolated from the fleeing multitudes,
she was left alone
on the lower slopes of Hoimun Mountain in Chŏlla-do.
After a week without food, she began to hallucinate.
With no milk in her breasts,
she mistook her baby, that was starving with her,
for a boiled chicken
and began to devour
the fruit of her womb.
She gnawed at feet and legs,
devoured the trunk,
the whole bloody mess.
And the baby bones.
Nibbled at the baby ribs.
Finally only the backbone remained.

Next morning she came to her senses
and searched everywhere for her little child
but all she could find was a backbone,
while her hands…her hands were caked in blood.

After that she grew insane
and went roaming the world,
laughing all day long.
She might well reckon this world
worth laughing at.

Volume 7 (1988)

Cho Bong-am

One day in January 1958
Cho Bong-am, chairman of the Progressive Party.
stood at the foot of the scaffold in Sŏdaemun Prison.

His last words were:
"Give me a cigarette."

Having been refused even one last cigarette,
thud! his two feet hung dangling.

Here, since his death,
faithful to his hope
at least in words,
"unification" no longer means invading the North,
    as Syngman Rhee insisted,
and saying "peaceful reunification" is no longer a crime.
But the day is still far away
when the shadow of his death will lift.

When his comrades went to jail
or came back out again,
that fine fellow
would donate a sack of rice
or a cartload of coal
and so give courage to that comrade's wife. A fine
  fellow, indeed.

Last night in a dream I saw Cho Bong-am, smoking
  a cigarette.

Lee Ki-sŏp

Two brothers from Saet'ŏ: Lee Ki-sŏp and Lee Ki-sŏng,
their names so nearly the same
that Ki-sŏp's mistakes
became Ki-sŏng's
and Ki-sŏng's doings
became known as Ki-sŏp's.
The one called Ki-sŏp
only felt happy if he beat someone up once a day
at school
or on the way home from school.
He'd spit in people's faces
picking a quarrel,
then
after a fight,
having pummelled, thrashed, kicked, stomped,
he'd put on airs and hide a sprained wrist.

Finally, having got a proper hiding
from Cho Nam-jik from Sae-mal,
he was left alone hitting the ground

and blubbering,
only that wasn't enough
so he peeled plaster off the mud wall as he blubbered.

He'd wanted to be born a wild dog or a wild cat
but in the end Ki-sŏp had been born a man.
He gave his own cousin Ki-yong twenty blows
for not sharing a rice cake with him.
Ki-yong hid the rancor he nourished,
then thrashed Ki-sŏp with a bamboo pole,
thrashed him across the shoulders
a good twenty blows.

After that Ki-sŏp no longer faced off with anyone,
became infinitely gentle,
until finally he'd stand faithfully for long hours
gazing at the western hills where the sun was setting.

So Ki-sŏp changed. In the end, he and Ki-sŏng
   died together
when the rightists were being massacred
as the communists were retreating.
Those brothers were caught among a group of rightists.

They were tied up and buried alive in a GI trench.
On good terms, they died
on good terms.

Their bodies were later disinterred and buried side by side.

My Elder Sister Chŏng-ja

Her eyes were inclined a little toward her nose,
so there was no telling who she was looking at.
Kim Chŏng-ja never lost her smile
spreading over her dimples.
She seemed born to smile.
When her skirt lifted, the sight of
the huge scar she had above her knee was repulsive,
yet she smiled at the sight of the hills in front of
    the village,
smiled at the sight of the hills behind.
Her skin was as smooth as smooth could be, so smooth
one of the sky's white clouds
seemed to have been her foster-mother
and she its foster-daughter.
She had lost her mother early on,
so from childhood
she cooked and washed and ran the errands
and all the while gazed at the white clouds above.
She would go the strawberry field
and pick strawberries which she gave me,
would go to the pine grove

and gather fresh pinecones which she gave me,
mushrooms too.
She'd teach me which were edible
and which you mustn't eat,
explaining that the ones you can't eat are mostly
    brightly colored.

As the wind rustled through the pines,
in my heart I secretly used to call Chŏng-ja,
who was five years older than me,
"Big Sister!"

A Green Frog*

No matter how bad the drought,
a green frog will never drink the water humans offer it.
It emits a drop of urine and leaps away.

There's a frog like that in Yongdun village.
Ch'ang-sul, the son of Kim Man-sik,
spurned the rice-cake a rich family's child offered him:
"Why should I eat left-over offerings
after your family's ghosts have had their fill? No way!"

The Ox

As the ox of our neighbors,
the family of Yu-t'ae and Pong-t'ae,
plods along
pulling their oxcart loaded full to overflowing,
if it feels like a shit
in front of some respectable house,
a spot where it doesn't know it should act respectfully,
it lifts its tail and lets go, *splish splash*,
all the time hauling its load.
The farm-help with the withered hand
that lives all the time with that ox,
drunk on cheap hooch
and feeling groggy,
calls out:
"Let's rest here a while."
He stops the ox
and pours a stream of piss
into the roadside grass,
no matter if girls are around,
or women,
or old folks, or anyone.

High in the air
swallows about to migrate are warming up.
Man, the sky's so blue, it makes you crazy.

Nam-sun

Nam-sun from Saemal
skips 100 times, 200.
All the kids have gathered,
all the grown-ups have gathered,
all the people from the upper village,
the middle, the lower village have gathered,
all the birds and weeds have gathered.
First she skips with eyes open,
then she skips with eyes closed,
skips 100 times, 200,
more, 250 times.

She'll kill herself.
She'll kill herself.

Brother and Sister Eight Feet Tall

In the days of Myŏng-jong, King of Chosŏn,
at the Han River harbor of Samgae
there was a porter eight feet tall,
a porter quick as a squirrel
even with thirty sacks loaded on his back.

And that's not all.
That porter's younger sister
was eight feet tall as well.
People at Samgae Harbor were amazed
seeing them hurrying off
backs loaded with thirty sacks.

But where is a girl like that
ever going to find a husband?
She's already getting on in years.
Finally,
one New Year's Eve,
after they'd lamented to their heart's content:
"Hey why don't you and me
set up house together instead?"

To which the sister replied:
"Sure."

So brother and sister, both eight feet tall,
became husband and wife.
Setting up an altar with a bowl of cold water,
from that night on they became husband and wife.

But things move slowly in this world
and it was three years later,
a full three years, before they realized
that a seed had entered the eight-foot tall girl
and was growing inside her.

They were obliged to flee by night, crossing
Mounts Weeping and Laughing in Kangwŏn Province.

Han Ha-un*

When the 1940s were nearly done and
I was in second year of middle school,
I was making the two-mile journey home
along a dusky path at twilight
trudging along
getting near the Mijei crossroads
when suddenly I noticed something lying
in the middle of the dark path.
My heart skipped a beat
then fluttered wildly as I picked it up.
It was a book.
A poetry book.
The poems of Han Ha-un, Korea's leper-poet.

"On and on along the earthen path…"

Once back home,
I read and reread it all night long.
I read the commentary too, written by a certain
   Cho Yŏng-am,
three or four times,

and the commentary by someone called
    Ch'oi Yŏng-hae too.

From that day on, I was Han Ha-un.
From that day on, I was a wandering leper.
From that day on, all the world was an earthen path.
From that day on, I was a poet — a sorrowful poet.

Chŏn Dae-sŏk

Beyond Okchŏng-gol Valley,
economizing on jackets of hemp or linen,
economizing on undervests,
Chŏn Dae-sŏk goes about naked to the waist
all summer long. No sense of decency!
"Women passing need only turn their eyes aside."
The local elders offer advice: "Look, Dae-sŏk,
won't you put on something when you walk about?"
His answer:
"What?
Why, skin is clothing enough.
Living this way
I never catch a cold all winter long."

And that's not all.
He makes his kids live naked too,
'cos living like that
they get no bills for flu shots, no medical expenses.

Two Generations of Thieves

That master-gambler
scares his son out of his wits:
"If you gamble I'll cut your hands clean off.
Never play with anyone who has bloodshot eyes,
don't even look at anyone with bloodshot eyes.
If you so much as see them
they'll infect you." Not only that,
he even forces his son to abandon his friends.

Shim Man-sŏp from
the steep hill in Haemang-dong, Kunsan,
has robbed several times already.
Now this time
after coming out of prison
he whispers something to his son Shim Chae-ku
and on arriving at a rich house
in darkest night
the father nips over the wall
while his son keeps watch.
The next time
the son opens the locked gate and slips in
while the father keeps watch.

Then
they carry the booty away on their backs,
take it all to the pawnbroker and turn it into cash.
When they've accumulated plenty of dough,
how can they help it?
"Let's have a bit of fun."
Off they go to the bar,
where father and son drink till they're stewed,
scarlet-faced. Then
they pretend to mend nets on Haemang-dong Wharf.

After a night spent weaving in and out of the meshing,
wow, their finger joints are all in a mess
or something like that,
and they talk nonsense.
From time to time, their nonsense
is drowned out by a boat's whistle.

Mother-in-Law from Seoul*

That venerable mother-in-law from Seoul over in Saet'ŏ
all too naturally
made her daughter-in-law go out in spring sunlight
then made her daughter go out in autumn sunlight.

With that kind of ill will she lived to be ninety-two.

Pak Il-ryong

Its mother had died, the new-born babe lay whimpering
but clung hold tight to life
and his dad Pak Tal-ho
cuddled the fretting new-born
as he went from house to house
around the neighborhood
and set about raising him with milk
begged from nursing mothers
in this house and that
and with water in which rice had been washed.
It was only in his third year of life
that he reckoned it safe to give him a name:
Pak Il-ryong.
He early grew used to the taste of barley,
sometimes even mixed with some scarce rice.
When the child smiled happily, he would exclaim,
"You dear little thing,
Il-ryong-a!"
And when he asked him to say "Daddy!"
he obediently said "Daddy!"

Hearing that fresh young voice
his father smiled proudly all around
as if boasting of having a bushel of rice,
as proud as he would be of a whole sackful of rice.

Il-ryong grew up on milk from several nurses
and later, when he was older —
how kind he was —
he used to go visiting the women who'd nursed him:
Mama!
      Mama!
           Mama!

Our mother's the first person to share something with us
and Pak Il-ryong had
one dead mother, of course,
but not just that —
he had five,
six or even seven live mothers too.
He was truly blessed!

After celebrating the rites for his dead mother each year
he'd take rice-cake around from house to house:
"Mom! taste some of this.

Mom! taste some of this.
                    Mom! taste some of this.
Here, poor dead Mom! taste some of this."

To-gil Bitten by a Dog

One young girl, Im-sun from Okchŏng-gol,
and one young man, Pak To-gil
from outside the West Gate,
fell in love, came close.
One day in a hollow up by the tombs
at the very top
of Im-sun's family burial-ground
To-gil grabbed Im-sun
and in a flash they were hard at it.
Then the dog that had followed Im-sun,
thinking its mistress was being attacked,
took a deep bite at To-gil.

When the wound on To-gil's thigh had healed
he used to boast:
"Look here,
look, what a love-bite!
Look!"

Only in the end Im-sun,
obeying her father,
married the son of the chief of Hoihyŏn county.
While To-gil
got spliced to a stout lass from Kunsan.

That stout lass often got a beating from To-gil.

Old Mister Mun

Old Mister Mun is the door-keeper at Kunsan City Hall.

He may seem to be dozing,
yet at the sound of the mayor's or a section-chief's shoes
he's on his feet in a flash
smartly saluting.
No matter how humble his social position,
there's a rule at his thatched house in Shinch'ang-dong:
when he comes home from work
his eldest son and his wife, with
elder grandson and younger grandson, all come
    trooping out
and last of all his elderly wife comes out.
Only his eldest son's wife is a bit less decorous:
she walks noisily, dragging her shoes.

Rising at early dawn, he shaves:
will he ever have white hairs on that rounded chin?
Then he eats his early breakfast
and sets off for work bright and early.

The City Hall yard is deserted,
but several mice run away, exclaiming:
"Sir!
    Sir!
Door-keeper, Sir! Mr. Mun, Sir…"
They twitter as they run.

Yuk-son

Yuk-son's the younger brother of Pang Sang-gil in Saet'ŏ.
He was born with an extra finger
that he uses with the rest.
In a flash he's holding up a straw sack.
You can't really consider him a cripple.
He's simply got one finger extra.
He's got one that's there when it's needed.

If someone throws a stone at him,
he spreads six fingers wide, and catches it neatly.

Volume 8 (1989)

Hundreds of Names

Kim Chŏng-hŭi of the late Chosŏn era,
Kim Chŏng-hŭi, also known as Yesan,

every time he wrote,
a new name came to mind
so he'd sign that work with a red seal
bearing that particular name.
He left 185 names.
185 names
still hidden in the shadow of the soaring hawk.

He was right. With every page written in his sharp
    jagged style,
the person who wrote changed,
so how could Kim Chŏng-hŭi be just one single person?

Changhang Wharf

The fellow who coils the rope from the boat
plying its trade between Changhang and Kunsan,
looks like the root of an arrowroot plant.
On being asked, he says he's in his forties,
but looks about twenty more.
He always smells of liquor,
and drinks his *soju* straight,
no snack to help it down.

If anyone notices and mocks him:
"How come you drink without eating anything?
The liquor will curse you, curse you,"
he replies:
"Don't you know that all the smells
from the mudflats of Changhang
are enough to help my drink go down?"

He may look like an elderly fellow
but when he ties the rope firmly
with his back bolt upright
he's strong enough to send the spray flying.

The Novice at Songkwang Temple

In the mid Chosŏn period,
when Buddhism was only practiced high in
   the mountains,
a mendicant monk heard that the head monk
at Songkwang Temple in Chogye Mountain
renowned in the Way, was encouraging monastic practice,
and came from the north to see him.
Below the temple, the river turns into a stream
and as he climbed up alongside the stream
a cabbage leaf came floating down on the water.
Seeing that, the wandering monk exclaimed:
"Why, I've come on a fool's errand.
What kind of virtue,
what kind of teaching
can I expect to find in a temple
that doesn't know how to treasure sacred offerings,
the goods of the community?"
And he turned tail, back down the way he had come.
Just then a little novice monk,
panting, came rushing down:
"Monk, Sir! Monk, Sir! Mr. Monk, Sir!

On your way up did you
happen to notice a cabbage leaf floating down?"
he asked with what seemed his final breath.
'Well, I did see one,
yes, and in that case..."
The wandering monk reversed his steps once again,
painstakingly
made his way to Samil Hermitage in Chogye Forest,
stood before the head monk's door
and requested instruction.
Just then heavy drops of rain began falling
from clouds covering the whole of Chogye Mountain.
The birds busily flew away.
The head monk's door opened.
And would you believe it,
the cute little novice he'd met just before,
who had come racing after the cabbage leaf, emerged:
"Why, rains come
                    and guests come.
Guests come
                    and rains come."

Blind Sim*

Up a back alley lives a blind man known as Blind Sim.
Actually, his family name is Kim,
but instead of Blind Kim people call him Blind Sim
on account of the famous legend.
Every evening, he goes out to the station
accompanied by his stick.
Standing forlornly in the station yard,
he grasps his stick first in one hand, then the other.

For a year and a half his only daughter, fourteen years old,
has been going out selling shrimp sauce
together with the neighborhood women.
Since Changhang wares are cheap,
by day she sells all she can carry on her head.
Then at nightfall she sets out for Changhang
and comes back home on the last train,
carrying a basketful on her head for the morrow.

When the train pulls into the station
and the few passengers alight,
Blind Sim's daughter is sure to be among them.

"Father!"
she calls out, in a voice like a rolling ball of jade.

Blind Sim's darkness is at once filled with light:
his daughter's voice!

"Are you back, child?"
"Yes, father."

No darkness anywhere.
The utter joy of the two together!
Light!

Sim Ch'ŏng

How could Sim Ch'ŏng be merely a girl in a tale?
How could Sim Ch'ŏng be merely a girl in a song?

Such a life! Such a death!
Hurling herself
into the sea at Indangsu in Changsan Bay,
her face enveloped in her skirts!
Surely she embodies the burning resolve deep in every
    Korean girl?

Rising again in a lotus blossom,
inviting all the blind people living here in darkness,
and in the midst of that dark dark dark
pinpointing her own blind father!
How could Sim Ch'ŏng be merely one faithful daughter?
Daughter of liberation,
opening the eyes of a millennium of blindness,
opening them to a bright new world:
such a girl is everyone's Sim Ch'ŏng, isn't she?

Volume 9 (1989)

Kim Chŏng-ho

Open the 22 volumes of the great map made
by Kim Chŏng-ho, also known as Kosan-ja, "The Man
  from the Hills."

Chosŏn's mountains twist and writhe.
Mountains soaring aloft,
mountains in harmony rank after rank,
mountains linked in chains,
mountains arrayed in fold upon fold,
and the folk who live below them are forceful folk,
as forceful as those mountains twisting and writhing.

Chosŏn's rivers twist and turn.
From the headwaters
sidestreams branch and meander
and flow away into the distance.
This land's rivers
never rest, you know.
Like pain
or like love, they meander on.

Born the son of a lowly soldier
in a humble cottage far from the capital,
he and his friend Ch'oi Han-gi
swore as young patriots
that Han-gi would master astronomy
while Chŏng-ho would master topography.

So he travelled the length and breadth of Chosŏn,
measuring hills,
measuring rivers.
He climbed to the top of the Paektu mountain range
and measured the sacred lake in the crater there,
came down
and measured nameless seaside hamlets
and thus
enamored of this land of ours
at last
he produced his atlas
in the reign of King Ch'ŏljong.
Aided by his little daughter,
he'd immersed himself in woodblock engraving
and produced his atlas.

At the start of King Kojong's reign,
he was condemned to prison,
perhaps by direct order of the Regent,
charged with having revealed the lay of the land.
It is even said he died in prison.
And, believe it or not,
his first map
and his ultimate atlas —
all Chosŏn's roads a criss-crossed net,
a point to mark off every ten *ri* —
ended up serving as the Japs' guidebook
during the Sino-Japanese war.

Alone, he'd undertaken
what the state should have done.
Alone, he'd dedicated his whole life to the task,
then disappeared from history.
As Ch'oi Han-gi testified,
his friend Kim Chŏng-ho
devoted himself to map-making from the age of twenty.
Examining these maps
long afterwards, you see
how truly rigorous and detailed they are.

No dates of his birth or death remain,
only Kim's great atlas has been preserved.
That is how it should be.
A true man leaves no trace.
A true task leaves its trace.

The Woman from Chŏng-ŭp*

You are better acquainted with our country's moon
than anyone since the days of Paekche!
Love extending everywhere
beneath the moon!

"Moon, rise now to the height of heaven.
Shine down to the farthest place, shine down.
Ogi-ya Ogang-jori
Ah Tarong-diri."

The Petticoat Thief

A thief broke into the kitchen,
hungrily gobbled up the left-over rice,
left a generous mound of shit
and then
rummaged through the dresser in the nearest room
and made off with one gold hairpin,
one calico suit
and two petticoats.

The next morning Kil-sŏp's mother,
the one who'd been robbed,
threw open the kitchen door,
curses pouring out as she cleaned up the shit:

"*Aigu!* You damned thief, like a sardine's guts!
What thief would steal petticoats?
Aigu! You petty-minded wretch, you dirty-minded rat,
Aigu, and you call yourself a man
with such wretched balls as yours?
Who ever stole petticoats from anyone's house?
Filthy piece of filth!"

Oh Sŏng-ryun

A revolutionary can't live under just his own name.
Each place he goes, he's someone else.
But certain revolutionaries, in the end
earn a particular name
as their destiny.
Among comrades, each with many names,
the revolutionary Oh Sŏng-ryun had five.
The name he was known by was Chŏn-gwang,
but he had four other secret names.

Second-grade Political Advisor
to the Chinese Communist Party's
northeast anti-Japanese forces,
then Chief Administrator of the Workers' Army,
he went into active service
and fought the Japanese.
He fought in more than a hundred battles,
expanded the range of weapons to include ideology.
He aimed at the enemy
and his comrades too.
In the end, one young fighter was heard to cry out:
"Leader Chŏn-kwang is my ideology."

In the so-called Kwandong Suppression of
    Red Guerrillas,
he disgraced himself by surrendering
to the Japanese search parties.
That was in the winter of 1941.

In the North Manchurian plains
and in Canton,
at Shanghai,
Bejiing,
and in the South Manchurian plains,
his commune
his hit-and-run attacks
his ideological infiltrations
his revolution — all was finished.
He betrayed the names of as few of his companions as
    he could,
but he betrayed the revolution as much as he could.
The Second World War came to an end.
After the Chinese Revolution, he was executed,
in the name of the motherland
for which he'd searched
wandering as a youth.

His baby son died of malnutrition.
His wife went missing.
Missing persons
are part of our land's traditions,
between revolutions and counter-revolutions.

The Liar

What would be the use of a world full of truth?
Just think how boring it would be
if there were nothing but truth in the world.
Isn't it as if there have to be lies
if truth is to be valued correctly?
Isn't telling lies from the age of three
what it is to be human?

Among such humans,
there are some who find lying so much more fun
    than truth
that they become truly expert liars.
Just look at Lee Hyŏn-bok from Taech'ŏn town.

As he went roaming about, doing odd jobs,
not only inside Taech'ŏn city limits
but throughout the Poryŏng district
and Sŏch'ŏn district,
everything he said was a lie.
If he said a place was five *ri* away, it was ten.

If he said So-and-So had died,
if he clucked with regret
and remarked that he was sorry they were dead,
invariably that person would prove to be alive.
Surrounded by a thick cloud of mosquito smoke,
keeping mosquitoes at bay with the smoke,
having caught a carp
and making a soup of it with tough pumpkin,
he'd devour a whole bowlful of barley-rice.

He couldn't endure not telling lies.
If people scolded him: "You have so much to say,
why do you choose only lies?"
what innocence he feigned!
Such perfect composure!
"When did you ever hear me tell a lie?"
was Lee Hyon-bok's invariable reply.

Politely greeting his father, old Nam-ku,
upon return from forced labor in some far-away place,
he said he'd performed the memorial rites for
    his grandmother,
although in fact he'd not done so.

Seeing no sign of fresh soil dumped outside the gate for
    the spirits,
his old father quickly guessed his son was lying
but he simply murmured:
"These are days when the living are starving,
so my poor family spirits
had better look in on some rich family's
    ceremonial offerings
and eat their fill there before coming back home."

His son might limp in one leg
and be a liar to boot,
a son is still a son
although he'd still not found himself a wife
though he was already forty.
Such grief that was, for sure, such mortification.

The Moon

Every time the moon rose, she prayed.
Finally Wŏl-nam's mother, at forty, bore a son.
In dreams before pregnancy,
she swallowed the moon.
After her son was born, Wŏl-nam's mother
would lose her mind
without fail
every time the moon rose.
Late at night, washing dishes,
she'd smash one bowl —
the moon then hid in a cloud
and the world grew blind.

Yung

His surname was Yung, of Puyŏ.

The son of King Ŭija of Paekje,
by the fourth year of his father's reign
he'd already risen to the rank of Crown Prince
but when Paekje collapsed,
instead of gaining the throne,
he was taken prisoner
and shipped off to T'ang Dynasty China.

But it seemed his fate was rooted in Paekje,
for he returned there with a Chinese fleet
and fought against Paekje's new army,
slaughtered many of his countrymen
and became the viceroy for China.
In that guise he ruled over Paekje.

Later he returned to China,
lived as honorary viceroy and finally died.
His father the king
and his younger brother P'ung

were both living in exile somewhere in China
but there was no way
he could go to be with his brother
or live with his father as a son should.

When fall came the only sound was monkeys wailing.

Volume 10 (1996)

Kim Dae-jung*

He was the embodiment of suffering
at a time when suffering was needed.

Kidnapped from a hotel in Tokyo
he was due to be butchered but escaped alive.
He was due to be tossed into the Straits of Korea
and become a water-spirit, but escaped alive.

By a narrow margin
he lost the presidential election of 1971.
His wave-stirring eloquence
shook crowds a million-strong, like an earthquake.
Alone, he was
a crowd a million-strong.

He made Park Chung-hee grind his teeth.

Even in the thick of the extreme suffering
in the early 1970s,
he stayed up reading all night long,
and often studied with an English tutor.

Everything was ready.
When he consulted with associates
he used to turn on the FM radio
to paralyze the hidden mikes.
And everything was ready.
Yet the one thing he hoped for,
the chance to become president,
was not yet to be his.

In all the crises that followed the coup by
    Park Chung-hee,
he never wasted the least moment of life,
not so much as a mustard seed.
As a result
no Korean citizen of the 1970s
could fail to know him, the most precise Korean of all.

Kim Su-hwan*

In 1969 he was the first Korean ever made Cardinal.
That scarlet skullcap was an honor, irrespective of faith.
But he is the humblest of men.
Throughout the 1970s
he never once gave vent to anger
yet was always strong.

He was not so much action as the key to action.

He used to sing like the young Virgin Mary
before she became pregnant with her Son:
There is a star in the sky,
there is a flower on the earth.

He holds within himself the quiet nighttime sea.
Sitting down with him,
suddenly dawn breaks.

He is truly molded of clay:
perhaps an earthenware crock
or a household storage jar?

Lee Ŭng-no*

In 1967, after he visited the North Korean embassy
in East Berlin without permission,
he was taken back to Korea,
to the Central Intelligence Agency,
to Taejŏn Prison.

Somehow or other
he managed to get paint and brushes in his cell.
He made do with scraps of plywood
4-by-6, the size of a book.

There he painted standing oxen.
They looked like anger quelled,
like fossilized erections.
He painted single flowers too.

At Taejŏn Prison the iron-barred window
in the cell for political prisoners
was covered with only a sheet of plastic
and it was well below zero inside.

If his hands were so numb
he couldn't hold a brush
he'd wriggle his fingers
then take up his brush.

Ultimately spring came. Flowers blossomed
on his plywood scraps.
After he returned to Paris
ink paintings arose on mulberry paper,
hieroglyphic ink paintings,
ink paintings of the endless masses,
one after another.

Dense clouds of steam arose
from his ponderous bald head.
Even in chill winter in the suburbs of Paris
his native land used to melt
into mud
like barley fields,
like larks above barley fields.

Yun Isang*

"Go: reveal the East!"
Such was the commandment he received
from the Dragon King below the sea.
So one wounded dragon was born.
So it set out.

That dragon came back as a prisoner
"invited" to the National Independence Day
    Ceremony.
That dragon thrust his head into the shackles
on the prison-cell walls,
used his last strength in a suicide bid,
refusing to let others murder him.
He wrote a final message with his spurting blood:
"My son, before history and our people
I am ashamed of nothing. The spying charge is
    a fabrication…"
At the very brink of death, his life was saved.

Then came the winter of life imprisonment.
In his cell, where his drinking water would freeze,
the dragon, shoulders hunched,

lay sprawled on the floor
wrapped in a blanket
dreaming of the butterflies of Chuang-tzu
on the banks of the Yangtze.
His musical scores survived:
rolling thunder
crumbling everything
into desolation.

The world outside Korea venerated his music
with full-dress reverence.
Could he perhaps be Mahler's successor?

The False Leper

During the April 3 Massacre on Cheju Island,
Chwa Sŏng-mo from Ponggae-dong
on the slopes of Mount Halla, a true man of Cheju,
completely plucked out the bushy eyebrows
shading his bright shining eyes.

Then, since that wasn't enough,
he crushed his toes with a rock
so he was able to escape
multiple arrests, multiple massacres
disguised as a leper.

Several years passed.
Still disguised as a leper
next
he was taken to the leper colony
on Sorok Island in Chŏlla Province.
He escaped, pretending to go to the latrine,
and disappeared into the blue.

His son grew up
but
every time he found himself a bride
he ended up being jilted,
suspected of being a leper himself
because he was a leper's son.

Father
father,
father, where are you?
All the tangerines are ripe. What to do?

Father.

Hermitage Poems

Among the 213 poems
left by Hŏ Nan-sŏl-hŏn,
among the 213 poems
remaining after she'd burned
everything she'd written,
there are 128 "hermitage poems"
celebrating her longing to quit this world.

She quit this life at 27
but still the pain expressed
in her poetry had lasted too long.
Her parents' family was branded as traitors,
her elder brother Pong suffered misfortune,
her younger brother Kyun was sent into exile.

A beautiful woman
always has to pay dearly for her beauty.
The harder life is
the more beauty is considered a sin.

So the world recites
poems produced by pain.

Poets from China
published an edition of her poems, that they praised.

Later
the Japanese poet Bundai
published a volume and loved to read from it.

What then is a hermit?
What then are hermitage poems
if not wisps of cloud born of a woman's pain?

Pak Ch'ŏl-ung

In the fall of 1977, as I was on my way
for an interview with the assistant governor,
going down one corridor of Sŏdaemun Prison,
I met a man so handsome, wow, he left you gaping.
I learned from the guard accompanying me
it was Pak Ch'ŏl-ung, under sentence of death.

The youngest in his family, Pak Ch'ŏl-ung
had organized his older brothers, killed
and buried a man and his wife,
antique dealers in Insadong, along with their driver.

Since he was under sentence of death,
he always wore handcuffs,
even in his cell.

That bright smile
those graceful movements
undoubtedly the star in some movie
only it was as if somewhere in his life

the seed of that dreadful act had sprouted
and grown up, taking his body for humus.

On the floor of the cellar
behind the necktie factory of the execution room
his sprawling corpse was neither evil nor good.

*Ko Sang-don**

He planted the Korean flag
on the summit of Mount Everest.
That twenty-nine-year-old man
and our national flag
stood there together.

It couldn't just have been strength.
It couldn't just have been will-power.
It couldn't have just been destiny.

That summit wasn't earthly.
Aeons ago
that summit was the celestial height
of all mankind.
In this world
long long ago, a twelve-year-old boy, Chu-mong,
escaped death,
changed his name from Hae to Ko
and founded a kingdom of thatch-roofed,
    wooden cottages.
He gave Koguryǒ its name.
Following him, here is

Ko Sang-don today
on the peak of Everest.
Now
he has nothing left to do
so long as all the Korean flags
out there to the east,
fly in the company of that flag
on the summit of Mt. Everest.

Notes

The Peddler of Bamboo Crates
Old Korea was full of traveling peddlers, with their goods loaded on a frame on their backs. In each town a market would be held, usually once in five days, where they would sell their wares. The Yalu River flows between North Korea and China.

Our Great-Aunt at Taegi
"*Aigu*" is the sound made by Koreans to express almost every kind of emotion, from deep grief to surprise and intense pleasure.

The Inn at the Road Junction
Koreans have always been accustomed to eating something while drinking. *Kimch'i* is the basic Korean side-dish, usually made of salted cabbage flavored with red pepper and allowed to ferment for a time.
The dead are buried wherever there is room, usually on the slopes of hills, with a circular mound of earth covering the grave.

Tears of Blood

Japan finally annexed Korea, after infiltrating its society for almost 20 years. A certain number of Koreans collaborated with the Japanese and are considered as traitors, including those named here. Lee Wan-yong was the Prime Minister when Japan annexed Korea. The occasion for the Russo-Japanese War of 1904 was Russia's refusal to withdraw its troops from Manchuria following the suppression of the 1900 Boxer Rebellion in China. Ch'oi Nam-sŏn and Lee Kwang-su ae recognized today as the two great figures of early modern Korean literary history.

Kojumong: The Founder of Koguryŏ

Koguryŏ was a prehistoric kingdom mainly located to the north of the Korean peninsula, in what is now north-eastern China, but also including northern Korea. Its main center later moved further southward, and it is considered to be the origin of today's Korea. (See also the last poem in the book.)

Lee Dong-hui's Wits

Kando is a name previously used to designate the

south-western portion of the part of China once known as Manchuria.

New Year's Full Moon
Koreans traditionally followed the lunar calendar, in which the year begins with appearance of the new moon of the first month (the "Chinese New Year"). Two weeks later, the first full moon of the new year was celebrated with special feasting, too.

The Wife from Suregi
Until children were born, a man's wife was usually designated by the name of the village she had come from, as here; once she bore a son, she would be known as "X's Ma." When food is being offered in ritual offerings for the dead, the souls are invited to eat by the main celebrant, who digs a spoon and chopsticks into a bowl of rice.

Hyegong: A Monk in the Days of Old
Hyegong and Wŏnyhyo may have taught at the same monastery for a time. Along with Chajang and Ŭisang, they are the most revered monks of the Silla dynasty (669–935). The call to monks to unite at

the end seems to refer to the violent conflicts and struggles for power between rival factions of Korean Buddhists seen in recent years.

No-More's Mother

In earlier times, it was the custom to hang a cord of rice straw across the entrance to a house where a baby had just been born. Pieces of charcoal were woven into it and, if the baby was a boy, red peppers too. Because only sons were entitled to make the offerings for deceased parents, the birth of a son was considered essential and sometimes a whole series of daughters might be born before the much-desired son appeared. In addition, parents had to provide a dowry when marrying their daugh-ters, which made the birth of too many girls unwelcome.

The Well

As noted, married women in Korea are still usually referred to by the name of their first child ("Pullye's mother"), never by their own name. In old Korea, lower-class women often had no name.

Man-sun

During World War Two, the Japanese military held an estimated 80,000 to 200,000 women and girls from a variety of occupied countries in sexual slavery. Many were recruited in Korea, often in the way suggested in this poem. The common euphemism, "comfort women," is a misnomer, of course, for they were subject to constant sexual abuse by the soldiers they were obliged to "service." Many were not even adults. The Japanese government still refuses to acknowledge that such women existed. Naturally many died and many of those who survived were too ashamed and too poor to return home after the war.

Kim Ch'ang-suk

On April 8, 1919, soon after the March 1st Independence Declaration, the Korean Provisional Government was established in Shanghai. Syngman Rhee, then headmaster of a school in Hawaii, was selected as its president and from the start was more interested in fomenting dissension than in forming a united front against Japan. Rhee was finally expelled by Kim Ku in 1925 for embezzlement. Until

1945 Rhee lived in Hawaii, claiming to represent Korea. The close links he had with powerful figures in the United States enabled him to become the first president of the southern part of Korea in 1948 and he kept that title until the massacre of students demonstrating for democracy on April 19, 1960 forced him to resign and quit Korea.

Uncle Yong-sul
A carriage and a pair is a little buggy drawn by two neat horses used for short outings, a sign of wealth.

Ŭisang, the Great Monk
Ŭisang (625–702) and Wŏnhyo (617–686) were perhaps the greatest Buddhist masters Korea ever produced. They lived during the Silla Dynasty (BC 57–AD 936), at the moment when Silla, with its capital city in present-day Kyŏngju, expanded its power to cover most of the Korean peninsula as United Silla (668–936).

Before setting out for China, Wŏnhyo spent the night in a cave. Groping around there in the dark, he found what he took for a gourd of fresh water, and drank with delight. In the morning he discovered that the cave was really a tomb, that the gourd was a human skull, and that the water was disgustingly polluted. This led him to realize the determining role of the mind in the nature of reality. He felt that he had no further need of going abroad to study, and studied his own mind instead.

Chih-yen is considered to have been the Second Patriarch of the Chinese Hua-yen School, Fa-tsang Hsien-shou became its third patriarch. Tao-hsuan founded the Lu-tsung school, the school of discipline.

Hua-yen is the Chinese pronunciation of the Pali word Avatamsaka, usually translated as "flower garland." The Avatamsaka Sutra is the longest and most complex of all the major Buddhist sutras and Ŭisang is reputed to have gained unequalled understanding of its fundamental vision of the unity of all things. (Ko Un has retold the concluding book of this sutra as *Little Pilgrim*.)

King Munmu (r.661–681) was the thirtieth king of Silla.

Wangsanak
The center of the ancient state of Koguryŏ lay in what is now China, just north of the Yalu River. Wuruk is reputed to have lived in the 6th century, in the kingdom of Kaya at the southern end of the Korean peninsula, and to have invented the *kayagŭm*. Both *kŏmungo* and *kayagŭm* are stringed instruments with long wooden soundboards. The strings of the former are plucked with a wooden plectrum, those of the latter are plucked with the fingers.

Lee Chong-nam
After Liberation (the end of Japanese rule, on August 15, 1945), there was almost no change in the manpower in police or administration, beyond the departure of the native Japanese. This caused strong resentment.

Old Jaedong's Youngest Son
Yukjabaegi is one of the fundamental Korean folksongs, improvised in a myriad of different ways depending on local or even family traditions.

Kim Sang-sŏn from Araettŭm
When a villager died, usually all the neighbors would offer to help carry the coffin in the village bier as far as the burial place.

Chin-su
Symbol of female virtue and faithfulness in love, Ch'un-hyang is the heroine of one of Korea's favorite folk tales, filmed by Im Kwan-taek in 2000.

A Traveler from P'yŏngan Province
Myohyang Mountain is in what is now North Korea.

Kushirŏng Pass
"Bitter resentment," known in Korean as *"han"* or *"wonhan,"* is the life-experience of constant frustration that leaves a spirit unable to rest in peace after death.

Yi Yong-ak
Like many Koreans of the time, Yi Yong-ak (1914–1971) went to study in Japan, eager to find a vision of modernity, and like many others he re-

turned more than ever convinced that the future lay in socialism. His writing reflected that conviction and he was imprisoned for it in South Korea shortly before the outbreak of the Korean War. He went North during the Korean War, hoping to find there the fulfillment of his dreams. It seems he survived until 1971.

Kim Ki-man from Mijei
Pyong = 3.9 square yards.

Im Yŏng-ja
The act of biting off the tip of the tongue and inhaling it in order to die of suffocation is a familiar way for Korean women to commit suicide.

Ssangga-mae
A double-crown refers to the presence on the top of the head of two whorls of hair instead of the usual one. This makes the hair stick out at odd angles, a problem for barbers.

Hong Chong-wu
Kim Ok-kyun was the leader of a group of young re-

form-minded officials in the later 19th century that became known as the "Enlightenment Party." After visiting Japan in 1881, he became convinced that Korea had to adopt similar reforms and open to the outside world. In 1884, the group attempted a coup against the conservatives then in power but it failed and he fled to Japan. In 1894, he was tricked into going to Shanghai where he was shot. His head was displayed on a pole in Seoul. The Imperial Association helped the Japanese prepare to annex Korea in the years before 1910, when the other Associations named were opposing the gradual Japanese takeover of Korea.

Wu-sik from Arettŭm
The day for spring offerings, known as Hansik, usually falls on April 5. Families visit the ancestral graves, repair any damage done by bad weather during the winter, and make offerings of food.

Yoi ttong is the Japanese expression corresponding to "Get set, go!" at the start of a race.

A Green Frog
It was commonly said that during the commemora-

tion rituals, when a table of food is prepared and "offered" to a family's ancestors, the spirits of the dead come and eat their fill. Once the ceremony is over, the family eat all that the ghosts have left, and also share the food with their hungry neighbors. Ch'ang-sul is being exceptionally proud.

Han Ha-un
This moment marks Ko Un's discovery of his vocation to be a poet. The first volume of poems by Han Ha-un was published in 1949.

Mother-in-Law from Seoul
High-class women avoided sunlight; a tanned face was a sign of low class.

Blind Sim
The famous legend referred to tells of a blind man named Sim and his daughter, Sim Ch'ŏng, who allows herself to be thrown into the sea as a sacrifice in exchange for rice, which she's been told will restore his sight if offered to the Buddha. It does not. Yet she is reborn inside a lotus bud and finally meets her father, whose eyes open when he hears her

speaking to him. The eyes of every other blind crea-
ture in the world open at the same moment. (See
also the next poem.)

The Woman from Chŏng-ŭp
This mysterious poem quotes lines from a popular
song, including the nonsense sounds comprising the
refrain of many such ballads. Paekche was an an-
cient kingdom in South-West Korea, the region in
which the town of Chŏng-ŭp is located.

Kim Dae-jung
This poem was written before Kim Dae-Jung be-
came President of Korea in 1997. In 1973, when
Park Chung-Hee had seized total power in Korea,
secret agents of his government kidnapped Kim
Dae-Jung and were about to throw him into the sea
until American CIA agents organized a dramatic in-
tervention to save him. The poet's choice of "pre-
cise" in the last line might seem puzzling; it suggests
that everyone else carelessly wasted time in those
years, by staying out of trouble or even collaborating
with the government.

Kim Su-hwan
Appointed Archbishop of Seoul before he was forty, Kim Su-hwan was made a cardinal almost at once. Ko Un stresses that this title is an honor bestowed by the Pope on certain key figures in the Church, who do not all bear witness to their faith in the very special way that Cardinal Kim did in the years of dictatorship.

Lee Ŭng-no
Lee Ŭng-no (1904–1989) played a major role in the development of modern art in Korea. Born in Korea, he studied in Japan, then worked to transform Korean art. In 1958, he went to live in Paris, where his style evolved in an increasingly abstract direction. After the notorious "East Berlin incident" recalled at the start of this poem, he spent two years in prison before returning to Paris. He remained critical of the dictatorial regimes and was never able to return to Korea before his death.

Yun Isang
The great composer Yun Isang (1917–1995) was kidnapped from his home in Germany by secret

agents of the Park Chung-hee government in 1967, brought back to Seoul, tortured, and sentenced to life imprisonment for treason. He was released in 1969, after strong international protests, returned to Germany and continued to compose and also to oppose the dictatorial regimes of South Korea. His works are widely recorded.

Ko Sang-don
Koguryŏ was a prehistoric kingdom located to the north of the Korean peninsula, in what is now north-eastern China. It later expanded southward, becoming the origin of today's Korea.

THE MARJORIE G. PERLOFF SERIES
OF INTERNATIONAL POETRY

This series is published in honor of Marjorie G. Perloff
and her contributions, past and present, to the literary criticism
of international poetry and poetics. Perloff's writing and teaching
have been illuminating and broad-reaching, affecting even
the publisher of Green Integer; for without her influence
and friendship, he might never have engaged in
publishing poetry.

2002

Yang Lian *Yi* (GI 35) [China]
Lyn Hejinian *My Life* (GI 39) [USA]
Else Lasker-Schüler *Selected Poems* (GI 49) [Germany]
Gertrude Stein *Tender Buttons* (GI 50) [USA]
Hagiwara Sakutarō *Howling at the Moon: Poems and Prose*
(GI 57) [Japan]

2003

Rainer Maria Rilke *Duino Elegies* (GI 58) [Germany]
Paul Celan *Romanian Poems* (GI 81) [Romania]
Adonis *If Only the Sea Could Sleep* (GI 84) [Syria/Lebanon]
Henrik Nordbrandt *The Hangman's Lament* (GI 95) [Denmark]
Mario Luzi *Earthly and Heavenly Journey of Simone Martini*
(GI 99) [Italy]

2004

André Breton *Earthlight* (GI 102) [France]
Paul Celan *Breathturn* (GI 111) [Bukovina/France]
Paul Celan *Threadsuns* (GI 112) [Bukovina/France]
Paul Celan *Lightduress* (GI 113) [Bukovina/France]
Reina María Rodríguez *Violet Island and Other Poems* (GI 119) [Cuba]
Amelia Rosselli *War Variations* (GI 121) [Italy]
Gilbert Sorrentino *New and Selected Poems 1958-1998*
(GI 143) [USA}

2005

Ko Un *Ten Thousand Lives* (GI 123) [Korea]
Vizar Zhiti *The Condemned Apple: Selected Poetry*
(GI 134) [Albania]
Krzysztof Kamil Baczyński *White Magic and Other Poems*
(GI 138) [Poland]
Nishiwaki Janzuburō *A Modern Fable* (GI 151) [Japan]
Maurice Gilliams *The Bottle at Sea: The Complete Poems*
(GI 153) [Belgium]
Takamuro Kōtarō *The Chieko Poems* (GI 160) [Japan]